PIPE FITTINGS

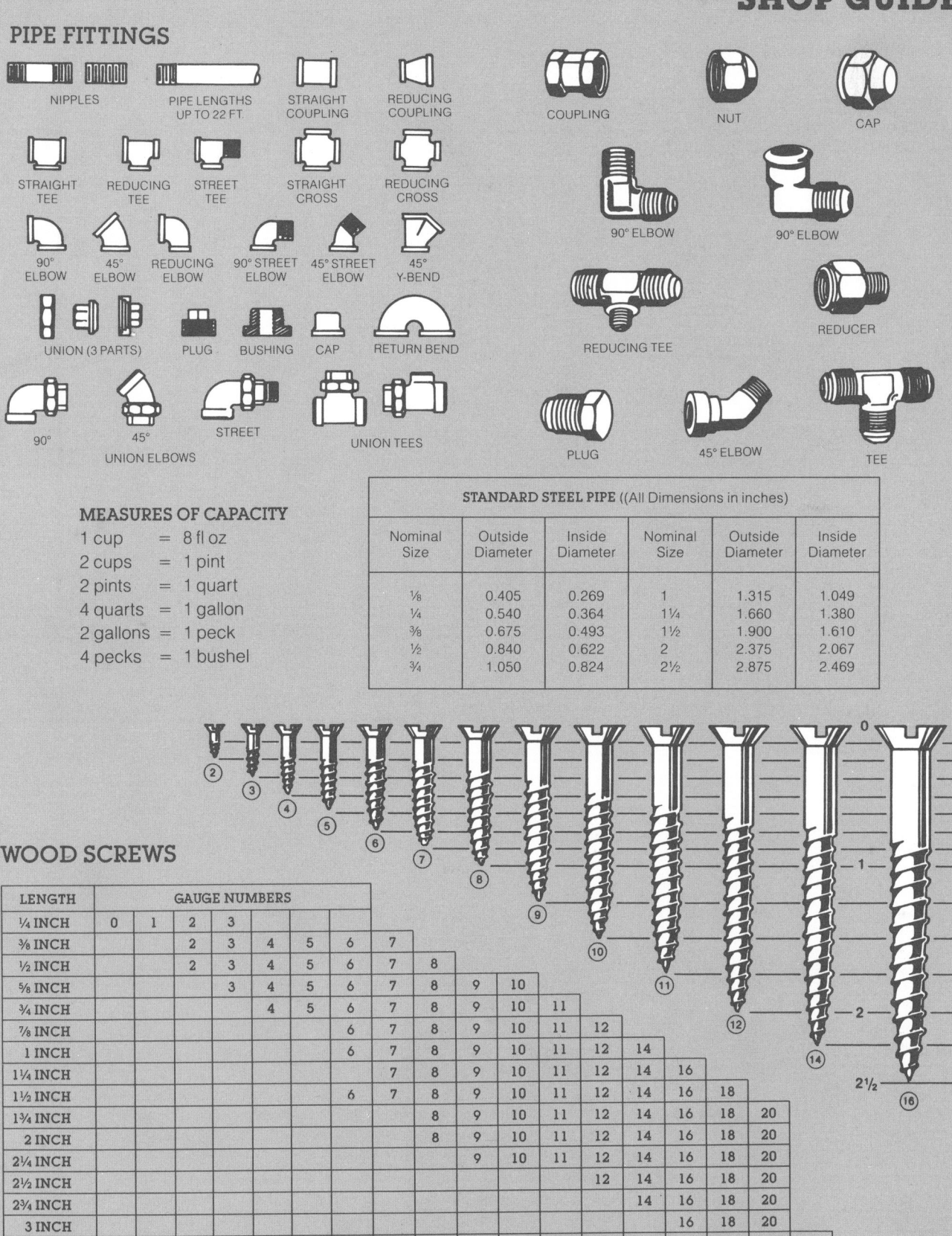

NIPPLES   PIPE LENGTHS UP TO 22 FT.   STRAIGHT COUPLING   REDUCING COUPLING   COUPLING   NUT   CAP

STRAIGHT TEE   REDUCING TEE   STREET TEE   STRAIGHT CROSS   REDUCING CROSS   90° ELBOW   90° ELBOW

90° ELBOW   45° ELBOW   REDUCING ELBOW   90° STREET ELBOW   45° STREET ELBOW   45° Y-BEND   REDUCING TEE   REDUCER

UNION (3 PARTS)   PLUG   BUSHING   CAP   RETURN BEND

90°   45°   UNION ELBOWS   STREET   UNION TEES   PLUG   45° ELBOW   TEE

MEASURES OF CAPACITY

1 cup	=	8 fl oz
2 cups	=	1 pint
2 pints	=	1 quart
4 quarts	=	1 gallon
2 gallons	=	1 peck
4 pecks	=	1 bushel

STANDARD STEEL PIPE ((All Dimensions in inches)

Nominal Size	Outside Diameter	Inside Diameter	Nominal Size	Outside Diameter	Inside Diameter
⅛	0.405	0.269	1	1.315	1.049
¼	0.540	0.364	1¼	1.660	1.380
⅜	0.675	0.493	1½	1.900	1.610
½	0.840	0.622	2	2.375	2.067
¾	1.050	0.824	2½	2.875	2.469

WOOD SCREWS

LENGTH	GAUGE NUMBERS												
¼ INCH	0	1	2	3									
⅜ INCH			2	3	4	5	6	7					
½ INCH			2	3	4	5	6	7	8				
⅝ INCH				3	4	5	6	7	8	9	10		
¾ INCH					4	5	6	7	8	9	10	11	
⅞ INCH							6	7	8	9	10	11	12
1 INCH							6	7	8	9	10	11	12	14
1¼ INCH								7	8	9	10	11	12	14	16
1½ INCH							6	7	8	9	10	11	12	14	16	18
1¾ INCH									8	9	10	11	12	14	16	18	20
2 INCH									8	9	10	11	12	14	16	18	20
2¼ INCH										9	10	11	12	14	16	18	20
2½ INCH													12	14	16	18	20
2¾ INCH														14	16	18	20
3 INCH															16	18	20
3½ INCH																18	20	24
4 INCH																18	20	24

WHEN YOU BUY SCREWS, SPECIFY (1) LENGTH, (2) GAUGE NUMBER, (3) TYPE OF HEAD—FLAT, ROUND, OR OVAL, (4) MATERIAL—STEEL, BRASS, BRONZE, ETC., (5) FINISH—BRIGHT, STEEL BLUED, CADMIUM, NICKEL, OR CHROMIUM PLATED.

P9-BBM-807

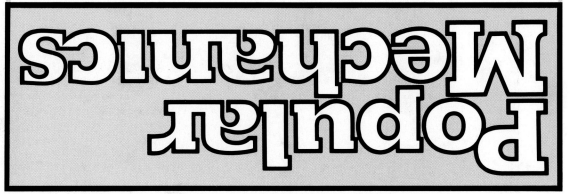

Popular Mechanics

do-it-yourself encyclopedia

The complete, illustrated home reference guide from the world's most authoritative source for today's how-to-do-it information.

Volume 1

❖

ABRASIVES
to
APPLIANCE REPAIR

HEARST DIRECT BOOKS
NEW YORK

Acknowledgements

The Popular Mechanics Encyclopedia is published with the consent and cooperation of POPULAR MECHANICS Magazine.

For POPULAR MECHANICS Magazine:

Editor-in-Chief: *Joe Oldham*
Managing Editor: *Bill Hartford*
Special Features Editor: *Sheldon M. Gallager*
Automotive Editor: *Wade A. Hoyt, SAE*
Home and Shop Editor: *Steve Willson*
Electronics Editor: *Stephen A. Booth*
Boating, Outdoors and Travel Editor: *Timothy H. Cole*
Science Editor: *Dennis Eskow*

Popular Mechanics Encyclopedia

Project Director: *Boyd Griffin*
Manufacturing: *Ron Schoenfeld*
Assistant Editors: *Cynthia W. Lockhart*
Peter McCann, Rosanna Petruccio
Production Coordinator: *Peter McCann*

The staff of Popular Mechanics Encyclopedia is grateful to the following individuals and organizations:

Editor: *C. Edward Cavert*
Editor Emeritus: *Clifford B. Hicks*
Production: *Layla Productions*
Production Director: *Lori Stein*
Book Design: *The Bentwood Studio*
Art Director: *Jos. Trautwein*
Design Consultant: *Suzanne Bennett & Associates*
Illustrations: *AP Graphics, Evelyne Johnson Associates, Popular Mechanics Magazine, Vantage Art.*

Contributing Writers: John Capotosto, *Old-time ice box,* page 58; Helaine Fendelman, *American antiques,* page 52; Roger Hammer, *Keep cool for less money,* page 32; *Airconditioning developments,* page 35; W. Clyde Lammey, *Sanding from start to finish,* page 16; Wayne C. Leckey, *Cutting compound angles,* page 50; C. J. Lindo, *Refrigerator tuneup cuts operating costs,* page 125; Tim Snider, *Appliance repair,* page 78; *Appliance basic checklist,* page 80; David A. Warren, *Angles: how to measure and cut them,* page 44; *Lincoln legacy: two mantle clocks you can build,* page 71; Ralph Wilkes, *Classic lap desk,* page 66.

Picture Credits: Popular Mechanics Encyclopedia is grateful to the following for permission to reprint their photographs: the Brooklyn Museum, page 55 (bottom left); William Doyle Galleries, pages 55 (bottom right), 56 (top and bottom left); Esto Photographics, Inc., pages 55 (top right), and 56 (center left and right); General Electric, pages 78 and 79; Heat Controller, Inc., Bud Healy, pages 36 and 37; Metropolitan Museum of Art, pages 53 (top and bottom), 54 and 55 (top left); Stanley Tools—A division of the Stanley Works, pages 44 (bottom), 45, 47 (top right, bottom left and right), 48 and 49.

© 1986 by The Hearst Corporation

All rights reserved. No part of this book may be reproduced in any manner whatsoever without permission of the publisher.

ISBN 0-87851-154-7

Library of Congress 85-81760

10 9 8 7 6 5 4 3 2

PRINTED IN THE UNITED STATES OF AMERICA

Although every effort has been made to ensure the accuracy and completeness of the information in this book, Hearst Direct Books makes no guarantees, stated or implied, nor will they be liable in the event of misinterpretation or human error made by the reader, or for any typographical errors that may appear. WORK SAFELY WITH HAND TOOLS. WEAR SAFETY GOGGLES. READ MANUFACTURER'S INSTRUCTIONS AND WARNINGS FOR ALL PRODUCTS.

Contents

VOLUMES 1-27

Boldface listings represent entries as they appear alphabetically throughout the encyclopedia. Additionally, each individual volume contains its own contents page with specific page references.

B

C

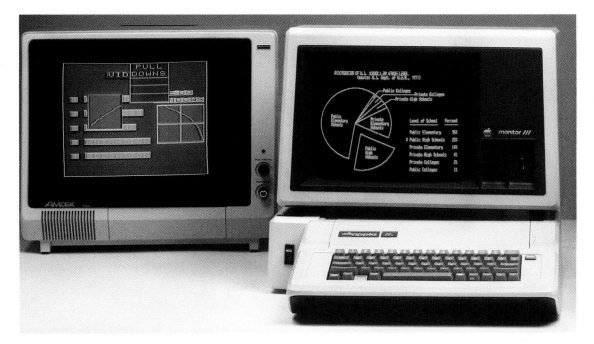

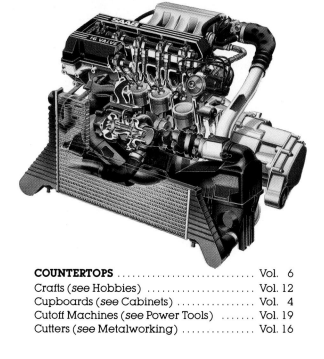

D

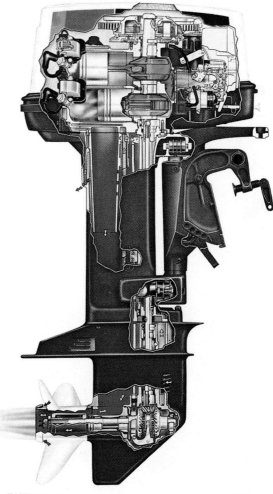

E

F

G

I

J

K

L

M

S

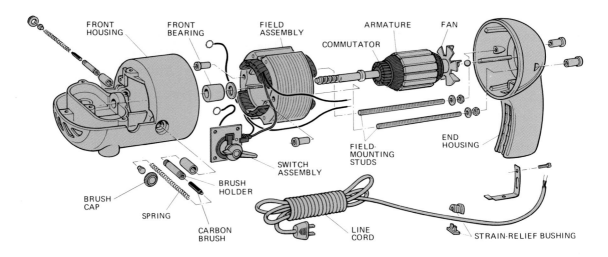

T

U

V

W

Y

Contents

Sanding from start to finish

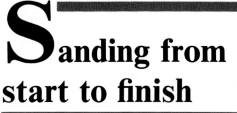

■ GOOD FINISHING begins with good sanding. On new work sanding brings out the best in the wood. On old work which has been previously finished, sanding should do two things: preserve the aged color of the wood and smooth the surface to take a new finish. Working from new-rough or old-rough is a repeat-step procedure, using sandpaper from coarse to fine through several successive steps. This applies to both hand and power sanding. In power sanding new work you may produce an acceptable surface in three successive steps. In hand sanding it may take as many as five successive steps, using five grades of sandpaper, to end up with a surface of equal quality. Each time over must remove the "scratch" marks of the step preceding; otherwise these marks will show under any finish.

On old work preservation of the color, or patina, of fine woods usually is desirable. Take off the old finish, either transparent or opaque, with a wash-off type remover. Then sand lightly with

PAD SANDERS, orbital and straightline types, are used mainly for the finish steps with the finer grades of sandpaper.

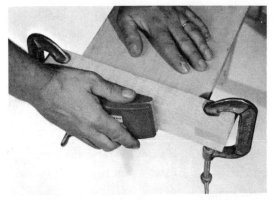

TO SAND end grain by hand, clamp waste strips to work as pictured. This not only keeps end square but prevents rounding edges. Or, alternatively, use an unpadded block.

UNPADDED sanding block usually saves time and work on rough surfaces. It cuts down high spots, sands out hollows and leaves a true surface.

"SHOESHINE" sanding is usually best for rounding corners and sanding turnings. Method maintains desired radius and leaves smooth surface.

a medium to fine grade paper and note results closely as you go. Don't use a hand scraper or power sander to remove the finish on old work when you wish to preserve the aged color. Finish with the finest grade of paper, normally 8-0 grade.

The best test you have of smoothness is simply to draw your forefinger lightly over the sanded surface diagonally or at right angles to the direction of sanding. Thus you can detect any minor depressions, or even slight roughness. Give these places, if any, a little more attention. But be careful not to cut through that old color acquired only by the aging of the wood.

New work can be handled a little more vigorously. If you are hand sanding and you discover any slight ups and downs on the surface, make a special sanding block from a 5-in. length of 2 x 4. Cut the ends at an angle of 5 degrees or so, cut a strip of sandpaper to the exact width of the block and to such length that the ends will fold up on the ends of the block where each can be attached with tacks. Don't pad with felt.

Purpose of such a block is to cut down the high spots, ridges and the like and level the surface the first time over. Use a uniform pressure, overlap each stroke about one fourth the width and be especially careful not to round the edges of the workpiece. Don't allow the block to overrun the edges more than about one-fourth its length or width. If there are knots in the surface, to be retained as a decorative feature of the grain, remember these usually are of a different texture, harder than the surrounding wood, causing the abrasive to cut somewhat slower. Such areas usually call for a few extra strokes in each sanding step to hold them flush. Keep a close watch when sanding certain softwoods having a coarse, flat grain. There may be especially soft areas which tend to cut down faster, producing a surface of low ridges and shallow hollows. Changing sanding strokes to a slight angle with the grain usually disposes of this problem. Keep

SOMETHING NEW in "sandpapering." Perforated metal forms edges that cut in all directions. Sheet is self-cleaning, removes stock very fast.

FOR BOAT-HULL sanding there's nothing quite like a portable belt sander of husky size with a belt at least 3 in. wide. It saves hours of labor.

USE A COARSE grade of sandpaper to bare wood after removing old finish, except on old work where you want to preserve age color, or patina. Use uniform pressure and don't allow block to tilt.

a close check on progress with the finger tip test.

Should the project you are working on be of veneer construction, either plywood or solid-core type, either old or new, be especially careful not to over-run the edges and cut down to the core stock. On new work the veneers used are likely to be quite thin, usually only about $\frac{1}{28}$ in., and may have already been machine-sanded, so you haven't much of the veneer left for the finishing steps. On older work the veneers are usually thicker, but as a rule they've been sanded pretty thoroughly when prepared for finishing.

One disadvantage of the unpadded block is its tendency to score the work more deeply than will a padded block and also it may tilt and slightly ridge the work along the length of the strokes if you don't keep close tab on the uniformity of the pressure you are applying. But it does level the work the first time over, cuts down the more resistant areas, such as knots and vertical grain, and in the end it's a timesaver. After using an unpadded block the first time over most craftsmen go to the padded block (the bottom of the block padded with felt or other soft, flexible material) or they use a flexible rubber block such as supplied by manufacturers of sand-

WITH FEW EXCEPTIONS, do your sanding with the grain, even though grain is at angle with workpiece.

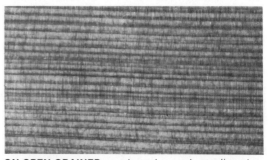

ON OPEN-GRAINED woods such as oak, sanding at a slight angle with grain will prevent enlarging pores.

FLEXIBLE rubber sanding block is often best for sanding surfaces originally in good condition. Care must be taken to apply uniform pressure throughout the stroke to prevent block from tilting.

HAND SANDING, medium to fine grade, is usually done with a felt-padded block unless surface is rough or ridged. Strokes should follow grain and overlap slightly as sanding progresses.

ON SQUARE PARTS with rounded corners a nylon abrasive pad or fine steel wool often gives that final finishing touch.

paper. Some even prefer to wrap the sandpaper around a piece of thick, hard felt for the final finish sanding. But in using flexible blocks of any type one should keep in mind that they have a tendency to round the edges and corners of any workpiece which is narrower than the block. For such work, also sanding end grain, a small unpadded block is generally best, especially if the finished job calls for sharp, straight corners with no waves or wobbles.

As a rule blocks don't work well on any type of curved surface that must be hand-sanded. Some types of straight moldings can be sanded quite accurately with flexible blocks but on moldings having irregular or curved shapes such as those on scalloped edges, one generally finds it best to cut sandpaper into small squares, fold once over and use the thumb or forefinger as the "block." Such a simple method is quite effective and much faster than one might suppose. Wear a glove or finger cot if there's much of this kind of thing to do.

The "shoeshine" method of sanding usually works best on turnings, either in the lathe immediately after turning to finish size or with the workpiece held in a vise, or on turnings already assembled, as in old pieces or unfinished furniture. Just tear or cut strips of cloth-backed abrasive from ½ to 1 in. wide, pass the strip around the work and pull on the ends in a back-and-

forth stroke. When sanding in this fashion in the lathe operate the machine at a slower speed and keep the abrasive strip moving back and forth and simultaneously along the work to prevent undue heating and discoloration of the wood. As a rule you use only the medium to fine grades of abrasives in shoeshine sanding, but you use descending grades from medium to fine to eliminate scratches as you go.

Only the bulb and vase shapes and the concavities of turnings should be sanded by the shoeshine method. Don't pass the strip over narrow beads as it tends to flatten them; use instead a fine V-file or 3-cornered file, touching it lightly to the work in a back-and-forth stroke and rolling it simultaneously to retain the curvature of the bead. In many cases a strip of sandpaper wrapped around a dowel of small diameter

FOR HAND-SANDING curves of short radius, sandpaper folded several times is quite effective. Flexibility of folded "pad" allows it to follow contour of surface without digging in or scoring too deeply.

DISC SANDER of swiveling type makes short work of truing a butt joint such as that pictured. Disc cuts very fast and leaves a smooth, swirl-free surface. Use only light, uniform pressure.

is handy for getting into flutes, round-bottom cuts, and on straight moldings where short-radius shapes are involved. Spread glue on the dowel and wrap the sandpaper strip diagonally with the meeting edges of the strip butted, not overlapped.

How to clean sandpaper

Sometimes there's trouble with the finer grades of paper clogging or glazing, especially on woods of resinous content, or on "oily" woods such as teak. Usually you can clean the abrading surface effectively with a brush having metal bristles; a brush of the type used for cleaning suede shoes is just the thing. When sanding old work preparatory to refinishing, residues of old fillers may tend to glaze the sandpaper and resist cleaning with the brush. When this problem develops just spill a little turpentine onto the work surface. This will usually cut the glaze and "re-sharpen" the abrasive. The turps will evaporate quickly and won't discolor the wood, but one should keep in mind that turpentine is rather highly flammable, that there is always some hazard in its use. Move the job outdoors when possible or have your home fire extinguisher handy. And don't smoke.

Once the initial rough sanding has been finished go to a finer grade of sandpaper, a grade that will remove the scratch marks of the first, and then continue the step-by-step procedure, going to a finer grade of abrasive each time, until the finger test turns up a glass-smoothness over the entire surface. Many craftsmen dampen the sanded surface after initial sandings from coarse to medium grades of sandpaper. Dampening the surface raises the grain, causes surface fibers to stand vertically, or near vertically. In this position they are easily cut off in the next step. On very fine work this procedure is often carried through several steps, to properly condition the wood for a "piano" finish.

Sanding by machine

Machine sanding with a portable electric sander is much the same thing except that it's faster and requires a little closer attention to control of the tool. Generally a portable belt sander is best for average work on flat surfaces, one having a 3-in., or wider, belt being somewhat easier to control when using fast cutting abrasives in the coarser grades. If the surface to be sanded is in reasonably good condition, no digs, gouges, dips, or ridges, then use of a coarse-grade abrasive may not be necessary. Make sure that the belt you use tracks properly when in place on the sander and be sure to check to see that it's running in the right direction. All sander

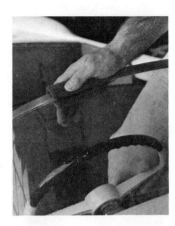

NYLON ABRASIVE PAD works on either metal or wood equally well. Just the thing for cleaning and "shining" up aluminum canoes, boat brasswork, door kick plates, or metal turnings. Fold or cut the nylon pad to a convenient size and use as you would sandpaper.

belts are marked with an arrow indicating the direction they are to be run.

Start the sander before lowering it onto the surface to be sanded and keep it moving after contact in slow, back-and-forth strokes much the same as in hand sanding, the strokes overlapping slightly and working either to right or left. Don't allow the unit to stop on the surface, even for an instant, and be especially careful to prevent it from tipping sidewise. If the unit is stopped momentarily, or permitted to tilt slightly, the coarser-grade abrasives can cut through thin veneers in the wink of an eye, or form a depression that's difficult to sand out. Just as in hand sanding with a block, be doubly alert to avoid over-running the edges and ends of the work.

Don't bear down on a belt sander. Usually the weight of the unit is sufficient to keep the belt cutting freely. If it seems necessary to urge it a little, as in sanding end grain perhaps, bear down only very lightly and keep close watch of results. Bearing down heavily may cause the belt to heat unduly and glaze, thereby greatly re-

ducing its efficiency. Once the surface has been leveled satisfactorily—use that finger test again —change to a finer grade belt, continuing to step down until you finish with the finest belt.

Pad sanders are of two types, the terms, or names, used referring to the action of the pad. In the orbital type the pad moves in a circular stroke. On the second type known as the straight-line sander the pad moves in a straight, back-and-forth stroke. On some later-model pad sanders the stroke can be changed from straight to orbital as desired. Pad sanders are generally used for the finishing steps with fine-grade abrasives as they are capable of sanding to a very smooth surface.

In general, stance is of some importance in both hand and machine sanding. Some prefer to stand at the side of the work when hand sanding as they can keep pressure and stroke more uniform on a relatively large surface. Working with a portable belt sander can be done in much the same position. Hand pressure is not necessary with the power unit, leaving the hands free to control direction and limits of the stroke. On some woods, especially those with a coarse, open grain, you'll get a somewhat smoother job by directing the strokes slightly diagonal to the grain through all the steps from coarse to fine. This will be true of both hand and power sanding. Also, it's advisable to do a little experimenting to determine the grades of sandpaper that do the best job from start to finish on a given wood.

Abrasive selection

■ THE MOST important thing to remember is that you must choose the *proper* abrasive. And that may be more difficult than it sounds. A manufacturer may call a particular sandpaper grit "Tough industrial abrasive—medium." Not much help. That term "medium" is hardly exact.

A veteran hardware-store operator with long personal experience will be able to prescribe precisely the paper you need. But how do you distinguish the person who speaks from personal knowledge from one who parrots all-purpose sales talk?

Two natural minerals

Almandite, an iron-aluminum mineral, is the one generally used for *garnet* grit in the United States. The bulk of U.S. almandite comes from a large deposit on Gore Mountain in the New York Adirondacks. It's reddish in color, sometimes orange, and does a better job than flint because its grains are very sharp. Heat-treating increases the mineral's natural hardness and toughness, but garnet still dulls too fast for metal working.

New synthetic grits

The "tough industrial abrasive" that manufacturers like to refer to is usually *aluminum oxide.* It's off-white to gray-brown in color, often with specks of black. Crude bauxite ore is purified, and titanium oxide is added for extra toughness, in making this grit. Crushing rolls are controlled to get the sharpest fragments. Makers then grade these for size and add them to the appropriate backing.

Aluminum oxide grit is chunkier than *silicon carbide,* but the silicon carbide crystals are the sharpest and hardest of the synthetic abrasives. Silicon carbide paper is iridescent black, often tinged with green. The crystals are generally considered less tough than aluminum oxide, although some tests do dispute that view. In any case, the silicon carbide cuts under light pressure faster than any other abrasive material.

There are a couple of other coated abrasives whose names you've probably heard: emery and crocus cloth.

Emery is a natural combination of corundum and iron oxide; its grains are blocky and cut slowly. They tend to polish the material being worked on.

Crocus is powdered iron oxide—rust. It's very soft and bright red. The value of crocus is in polishing operations where you want to remove only the very minimum of stock.

How rough is 'medium'?

In selling to the general public, the coated abrasives industry tends to rely on the terms *fine, medium,* and *coarse* instead of being specific. (Carborundum also uses the terms *extra fine* and *super fine.*) Even those manufacturers who use numerical designations sometimes stick with such old symbols as ½ or *6/0* or *1G*—meaningless until you've learned their particular code.

The various grade systems don't match. Take 180-mesh grit. Depending on the system being used, it might be called *3* or *3/0* or *5/0* or *extra fine.* All can indicate the same grit size.

But mesh numbers classify all grits by the openings per inch in fine silk screens used to sort them. The 22 screens range from 12 openings per inch to 600. The grade-mesh table shown here translates various grading terms into the mesh-number system.

CLOSED-COAT PAPER (left) has abrasive over entire surface for fast cutting. Open coat (right) has less coverage, won't clog as fast.

Technical Grades		Simplified Grades		Other Grades	
Aluminum Oxide Silicon Carbide Garnet & Flint					
Mesh	Symbol	Flint	Emery	Flint Finishing	Emery Polishing
600					4/0
					3/0
500					2/0
400	10/0				0
360					
320	9/0			7/0	1/2
280	8/0			6/0	
240	7/0			5/0	1G
220	6/0	Extra Fine		4/0	2
180	5/0		Fine	3/0	3
150	4/0			2/0	
120	3/0	Fine			
100	2/0		Medium		
80	0	Medium	Coarse		
60	1/2				
50	1		Extra Coarse		
40	1 1/2	Coarse			
36	2				
30	2 1/2	Extra Coarse			
24	3				
20	3 1/2				
16	4				
12	4 1/2				

THE SAME terms may indicate a variety of grit sizes, depending on the abrasive material used. This chart decodes the common terms. The mesh number is the most precise. It tells the number of threads per inch for a screen that will pass a particular size grit material.

Some manufacturers still show mesh grades only on products for industrial customers. Still, mesh numbers are taking over, if slowly. Learn to use them. Know what number 80 or 120 or 180 paper does for you. Then you can rely on numbers instead of advertising adjectives. If you can't find specific data on the package, it may be on the back of the paper itself.

Industry people who resist citing mesh numbers explain that slightly different grit sizes can give almost identical results: 80-grit paper with the continuous stroke of a disc sander or 90-grit paper with hand sanding or 100-grit paper with the short strokes of a vibrating sander all can produce about the same finish. Thus the different numbers might be confusing, they say.

Choose a protective package

The package has other importance when you're shopping for sandpaper. Many of us discard a coated abrasive after only a bit of its productive life. If you choose the paper carefully, you should also pick one of the packages that serve to protect the supply for re-use. A stiff cardboard envelope with a hole from which to hang it is one handy form. But be sure to store it in a dry place. Humidity ruins sandpaper.

The *backing* is nearly as important as the grit. The backing has to hold together if your paper is to have any staying power. Generally, today's papers do a good job. But strong backing is especially important for machine sanding, whether you're using a disc on a portable drill, an orbital sander or a belt sander.

Available in four weights

The paper comes in four weights: A, C, D, and E. Few specialists feel A has much value, although it's likely to be the backing for bargain flint. Discs cut from A-weight paper are likely to give up without much fight, and the clamps of a vibrating sander may well tear it. C- and D-weights do a better job and E is as heavy as paper backing comes—more than three times as heavy as A-weight. E is commonly used on commercial floor-sanding machines.

Cloth backing is also available, in two weights. J-weight is the more flexible while X is stronger and more durable.

"Fibre" backing, actually a hardened rag-stock paper, has more body than any other backing. It's sometimes combined with either cloth or ordinary paper. Those combinations are usually for industrial use, however.

Even with good backing and the right range of grits, certain jobs can give your trouble. Loading, in which the stock being removed (swarf, it's called) fills the spaces between grit particles, is frustrating. When the spaces between grains load up, the sharp edges can't reach down and cut as they should.

An answer to loading

A standard approach has been to use open-coat paper, in which 30 to 50 per cent of the backing's area is exposed, carrying no grit.

Special anti-loading treatments are a recent development. A particular chemical, usually zinc stear- ate (from soap family), covers grit and all. In use, the edges cut through it instantly, but the rest of the coating gives the swarf no grip.

You can doctor your own sandpaper similarly. Just rub a bar of soap across the grit. But think ahead. The soapy compound has to be removed before you paint or otherwise finish the surface. Unless you plan further sanding anyway, you might well stay clear of the soap.

What Carborundum calls Sand Screen is a still newer response to loading. This material is open-mesh plastic screening coated with aluminum oxide or silicon carbide grit. Such products from 3M are called Wetordry Fabricut; from Norton, Screen-Bak; and from Armour, Abrasive Screen Cloth.

Carborundum people are enthusiastic: "It's great for something like sanding that gummy anti-fouling paint from a boat hull. When this stuff starts to load up, all you do is slosh it around in a bucket of water. The go back to sanding."

Buy paper in bulk

If you have lots of sanding to do, buy the paper in bulk. Paint stores often sell a dozen sheets for the price of 10. For a big job, buy what the industry calls a "sleeve"—50 or 100 sheets, depending on the grade. Don't forget the need for careful storage, however.

How about steel wool for woodworking? Some experts find it messy and prefer sandpaper. Others agree, though at least one experienced hardware man sees an exception: "Use 0-0-0 steel wool after each coat of polyurethane and the finish will be like glass," he says.

Steel wool comes in seven grades. From fine to coarse, they are 0-0-0-0, 0-0-0, 0-0, 0, 1, 2, and 3. Steel wool is almost identical regardless of brand. You may as well shop for price.

With abrasives as with the rest of your shop equipment, pick the right materials and use them right. You'll end each job with a smooth finish!

Using abrasives

■ SANDING IS ONE of the most common construction and repair tasks performed around the home and shop. It's also one of the easiest. But unless you select the correct abrasive and use it properly, you'll have a hard time achieving good results.

To begin with, sandpaper, or "coated abrasive" as it is technically known, is identified by three things: the type of abrasive particles on its surface, the grit (or coarseness) of the particles and the actual amount of abrasive on an individual sheet. Your choice depends on the work you are doing.

Two of the most common sandpapers are flint and garnet. Flint is less expensive than garnet and thus is the logical choice when you're sanding surfaces that clog the paper quickly and spoil it such as soft, gummy woods, or when you're removing paint and other finishes. Garnet is tougher and longer lasting and works better for sanding all types of hardwoods.

The closest thing to an all-purpose abrasive is aluminum oxide paper. It can be used on wood, metal, plastics and fiberglass. Its abrasive coating is the same material used in grinding wheels, so it's very durable and holds up well when used in power sanders.

Silicon carbide is the hardest abrasive generally available for consumer use. Its particles are nearly as hard as a diamond, so it's ideal for sanding nonferrous metals, composition boards and plastics. It can also be used with water or mineral oil for rubbing down varnish, polyurethane and lacquer finishes, as shown in the photo.

The grit of an individual sheet of sandpaper is identified by the number on its backing. These numbers range from a very coarse No. 12 to a superfine No. 600, with 22 increments between. The finer papers frequently are available with cloth backings as well as the standard paper back. The cloth is more flexible and better for sanding curved shapes.

On many abrasives, you'll also have a choice between closed and open coats, which indicate how many particles are on the surface of an individual sheet. Closed coat means coverage over the entire sheet, while open coat indicates 50 to 70 percent coverage (see photo). Open coat does cut slower, but it won't clog as quickly.

WHEN SANDING WOOD, work with grain (left), not against it (right). Latter yields deep scratches. Same grit was used on both boards.

WHEN SANDING ROUNDED CORNERS and contours, abrasive works best if it's backed with resilient block. Padding allows the paper to conform to workpiece's shape.

TO SAND SCULPTURAL SHAPES, cut cloth-backed abrasive into narrow strips and use like a shoeshine rag. Paper-backed abrasive will work if you apply masking tape to back.

SANDPAPER CAN ALSO BE USED to achieve a true flat edge with the aid of two straight-edged boards clamped to the workpiece as shown. Use an unpadded sanding block.

FOR RICH LUSTER on finish coat of varnish or polyurethane, use waterproof silicon carbide paper, available in grits from 360 to 600. Use water or mineral oil as lubricant.

FOR FINAL SANDING on irregular shapes such as the molding shown, use a nonwoven nylon fiber pad in medium or fine grit. These are often sold for cleaning kitchen pots.

Stick with the right glue

■ CHOOSING THE right glue—and handling it right—will hold your work together. That may seem an obvious statement, but modern adhesives will keep nearly anything together—from buildings to airplanes.

Bear in mind, however, that no one glue will do everything. You have to know which is best for what.

Actually there are only about a dozen basic types of glue. The question of which one to select will depend on the specific characteristics of the glue and the nature of the job. Many glues are quick-setting, while others are not. Offhand, a quick-setting adhesive would seem to be ideal and so it is—for small assemblies. But what happens when a quick-setting glue is used on a large, complex assembly?

Trouble. It may be difficult to get all the necessary surfaces joined together before the glue on some joints begins to dry. It may well start to dry before you can apply clamping pressure, or even before all the surfaces are ready.

Warmth—whether of the air, the glue, or the material to be bonded—makes such problems more likely. Whether an adhesive depends on a chemical reaction or simply on the evaporation of its medium, almost any adhesive sets faster at higher temperatures. That's why some craftsmen put the glue container in a larger container and surround it with ice.

Tight fit—or loose

The fit of a joint can also influence your choice of glue. Most glues work best when surfaces match well. For joints that don't mate perfectly, a glue with good gap-filling properties is the obvious choice. Sometimes joints *must* be loose-fitting so the work can be assembled. Projects with dowel or mortise-and-tenon joints that angle toward or away from each other often re-

quire joints that are loose. The glue must fill the gaps.

Moisture and heat resistance

How about moisture resistance? Can you get by with a water-resistant glue or must you have one that's waterproof? It depends on the outdoor project you're working on, how much it will be exposed to the elements.

A chair put together with water-resistant glue will serve nicely on a covered porch, but the same chair would require waterproof glue if used out on the lawn or open patio.

Still another factor to consider in glue selection is its resistance to heat. Thermoplastic glues like the popular white polyvinyls become soft at temperatures above about 150° F. Such glue would be a poor choice for a project such as a

CHOOSE THE GLUE FOR THE JOB

KIND	USES	GAP FILLING	STRENGTH	WATER RESISTANCE
Hide (animal)	Structural bonding of wood: indoor furniture, cabinets, veneer. Available as liquid.	Good	High	Poor
Casein	Structural bonding of wood for most applications; particularly good for oily woods such as teak, lemon, yew. Can be used at any temperature above freezing. Mix powder, water.	Good	High	Fair
White (polyvinyl resin)	All-around household and shop glue for furniture making and repair, model and hobby work, paper and leather. Ready to use.	Poor	Medium	Poor
Aliphatic resin	Structural bonding of wood for furniture assembly, casework: edge and face gluing. Ready to use.	Good	High	Poor
Plastic resin	Structural bonding of woodwork where considerable moisture resistance is desired. Mix with water.	Poor	High	Good
Waterproof resorcinol resin	Structural bonding of wood exposed to soaking: furniture, framework, boat building and repairs. Two components.	Good	High	Excellent
Contact cement	Nonstructural bonding of wood, paper, fabrics, glass, cork, felt, linoleum. Laminating veneers and plastic compositions (Formica, Micarta and so forth) to countertops and vertical surfaces. Ready to use.	Poor	Medium	Very good
Epoxy resin	Structural bonding of rigid materials: wood, metal concrete, brick, tile, glass, china, some plastics and any application requiring high strength or extreme outdoor exposure. Two components.	Good	High	Excellent
Hot melt (glue gun)	Bonding wood, metal, leather, fabrics, plastics. Household repairs, hobby and craftwork. Ready to use.	Good	High	Excellent
Mastic adhesive	Installing plywood and hardboard paneling, gypsum wallboard to wood, plaster, concrete. Bonds ceiling and wall tiles, floor tiles. Ready to use.	Very good	Medium	Excellent
Silicone seal	Bonding glass, metal, pottery, porcelain: aquarium construction, weatherstripping, caulking. Ready to use.	Good	Medium	Excellent
Super glues*	Bonding glass, metal, wood, rubber and numerous other nonporous materials. Ready to use. *A wide variety is available. Check labels for specific applications.	Poor	High	Excellent

GLUES THAT require mixing must be measured carefully; a postal scale can help. Mark measuring cups and spoons so you don't accidentally contaminate one component with the other.

END GRAIN soaks up glue fast, so it should get two coats. Give it a thin coat first, add glue to the mating surface, then recoat the end grain before joining pieces.

NEWLY GLUED surfaces are slippery. Start a few nails through a butt joint before applying any glue. Projecting points will grab the mating piece as the two join, preventing skidding.

TEMPORARY CLEATS help ensure that you space shelves accurately. After you lay a bead of glue, spread it with a brush to be sure you have glue distributed evenly along the joint.

ON ANY JOINT, a larger gluing surface means stronger construction. Lap joints, dadoes, and tongue-and-groove joints are among those that offer extra gluing-surface area.

SOME IRREGULAR assemblies are nearly impossible to clamp. Select a fast-setting glue such as 5-minute epoxy so your hands—with a steady grip—can substitute for clamps.

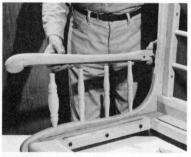

PARTS YOU will have to nurse into place can't have tight-fitting joints or fast-setting glue. Make the joints a bit loose and use a gap-filling, slower-setting glue.

WHITE GLUE cut half-and-half with water is excellent for sealing edges of plywood that will be painted. It prevents the grain on the edges of the plies from showing through.

HOT GLUE from an electric glue gun provides quick stick for a variety of craft jobs and do-it-yourself projects. You'll find it handy in gluing together parts of models.

radiator enclosure or something that will be placed near a furnace.

Follow directions

These are examples of the considerations you should keep in mind while you decide which glue to use. The projects you work on will indicate others. Be sure to check the manufacturer's in-structions thoroughly and follow them to the letter. Manufacturers want glue to perform in a way that satisfies you, and instructions are written with that in mind.

Several of the more powerful adhesives require mixing by the user. Accurate measurements are important. When a powder is to be mixed with a liquid (sometimes water) and pro-

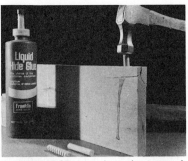

HAMMER TEST shows how glue trapped at the bottom of a hole can split the work under clamping pressure. Always plane a flat on a dowel for such jobs, giving excess glue an escape route.

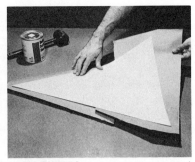

PAPER SHEETS keep contact-cemented surfaces apart as you position them. As the sheet comes out, the exposed, glue-laden surfaces grab each other firmly. There's no reconsidering!

SUPERGLUES can bond wood trim, even to slick plastic laminates, without nails or clamps. But check the label; some don't work well on particular kinds of surfaces.

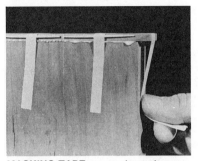

MASKING TAPE can replace clamps in gluing edge strips. Toothpicks at the strip's edge take care of glue squeezing out. Slightly larger pieces of scrap will give more clearance.

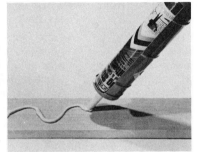

MASTIC ADHESIVE works great when you're installing furring strips on a concrete wall. If the original wall is uneven, however, big blobs from a can will do a better job.

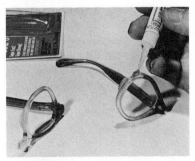

FAST SETTING and strong, some new superglues can even repair eyeglass frames. But some don't work on particular kinds of plastic; check the label in advance.

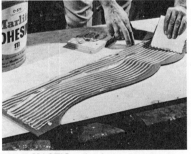

BULK MASTIC adhesives are more economical on large jobs like putting up sheets of paneling. A serrated tool lets you spread it evenly, yet assures you're using enough.

SPRAY ADHESIVE is a great way to stick fabric to wood. Coat both surfaces and let them set a moment or so before joining them. It gives you new decorating possibilities.

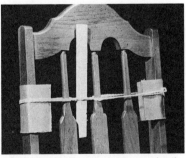

A TOURNIQUET or sometimes a simple strap will help when other clamps don't offer much. For furniture, a glue that swells wood fibers locks parts together securely.

portions are by volume, you'll be wise to "fluff up" the powder first to get an accurate reading on the volume. When proportions are by weight, a postal scale is handy.

Be careful not to contaminate your stock of one element with traces of another. Old craftsmen often use a pair of teaspoons that have been retired from active table service. They paint the handles with contrasting colors to avoid interchanging them by accident.

Kinds of glue

● **Polyvinyl (white) resin glue** is a good all-around household and workshop glue for furniture repairs. It sets fast at room temperature, dries clear leaving an invisible glue line, and can be used for paper, leather and cork as well as wood. It's quite strong, but softens under heat and is not waterproof. White glue also doesn't handle sanding well; wipe off what squeezes out—promptly.

• **Liquid hide (animal) glue** is an old-time favorite in the furniture industry. It's made from bones, hooves and hides of animals, makes a tough, lasting bond, has excellent gap-filling properties and is very slow-setting. This makes it ideal for large assemblies.

A disadvantage is that it is not waterproof. Hide glues lost some popularity for a while with the coming of the synthetics, but are now making a comeback. The availability of hide glue as a liquid has helped broaden its acceptability. Originally it was available only as sheets or flakes. You had to soak it until it dissolved and keep it hot until it was applied and quickly clamped. Some users also found the aroma unappealing.

• **Casein glue** is made from mild curd, hydrated lime and sodium hydroxide. It is available in powder form and is mixed with water for use. It can be used at any temperature above freezing, has good strength and is fairly water resistant. It is very abrasive to tools and will stain some woods such as redwood. It is especially effective on oily woods such as teak and lemon. It is good as a gap-filling glue.

• **Plastic-resin glue** is a dry powder made with urea resin. The catalyst or hardener is incorporated in the powder. It is mixed with water to a creamy consistency for use. Highly water-resistant and stain-free, it sets very hard to produce a bond stronger than most species of wood. It's a good choice for salad bowls, serving trays and other articles subjected to moisture. Joints must be well fitted, however, because this glue is a poor gap-filler.

• **Aliphatic resin glue,** a relative newcomer among the synthetic resin glues, is a creamy, light tan liquid and comes ready to use. It is somewhat similar to polyvinyl white glue but has decided advantages. It is strong, highly resistant to heat and takes sanding very well. It's a good gap-filler, actually holding better in a thick glue line than in a thin one. But it isn't waterproof.

• **Resorcinol water-proof glue** is a two-component adhesive. When the wine-colored resorcinol resin is combined with the dry-powder catalyst, it cures at room temperature. It is 100-percent water-proof; it will withstand extreme cold as well as boiling water, acids, alkalies and solvents; and it is excellent for building or repairing boats, outdoor furniture and toys. It is quite expensive, leaves a dark glue line, is slow-setting and fills gaps rather well. But it cannot be used below 70° F.

• **Contact cement,** a neoprene-based, ready-to-use liquid, is an excellent adhesive for bonding plastic laminates to plywood. Also recommended for joining combinations of wood, cloth, cork, leather, ceramics and thin metal. It is applied to both surfaces and allowed to dry for about 30 minutes before assembly. The parts bond immediately upon contact and require no clamping. The regular type is highly flammable and must be used with good ventilation and no open flame. A nonflammable, latex-base type is also available for use where a fire hazard exists.

• **Hot-melt glue-gun glue** is a remarkably handy household and shop adhesive. Special adhesive cartridges in stick form are inserted into the chamber of the electrically heated gun and provide the quickest and easiest method of bonding two surfaces. You simply press to squeeze out a bead of hot melted adhesive that sets in 60 seconds.

The glue sticks to almost anything except a few stubborn plastics. It is, completely waterproof and works well as a gap-filler in loose joints. A caulking cartridge is also available for use in bathrooms, outside the house and on boats, autos, concrete, vinyl pool liners and inflatable toys.

• **Multi-resin hot-melt glues** don't depend on a glue gun; they're often sold in foil trays. You melt the glue on a hot plate or similar device. Such brands as "Hot Grip" bond to plastics that defeat other adhesives.

• **Epoxy resin adhesive** is a two-component resin and catalyst material that produces a very strong waterproof bond. Equal amounts of resin and hardener are mixed together for use. Many epoxies are available with curing times ranging from five minutes to more than one hour. All have excellent gap-filling properties. Most will work even on wet lumber—especially advantageous on outdoor construction where thoroughly dry lumber is rare. Another plus: Odd-shaped fabrications practically impossible to clamp are easily put together with fast-setting epoxy. Ordinary hand pressure for a few minutes does the trick.

Measuring equal amounts of the two components is made easier by new packaging methods. The two are marketed in what functions like a double-barrelled tube. A single key at the rear squeezes both tubes equally so equal amounts are automatically extruded.

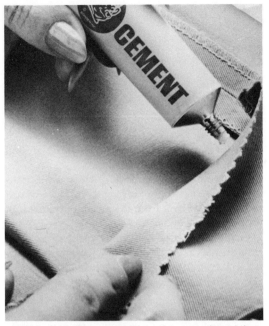

FABRIC CEMENT such as Elmer's is water-based, but is said to be laundry and dry-cleaning safe. Besides helping seamstresses, it works on leather, canvas, fur and other fabrics for craft and hobby projects.

WINDSHIELD SEALER forms a clear, tough, flexible film that holds glass to synthetic rubber, stainless steel, aluminum and wood. The fast-drying material is water-based, but still is water-resistant.

Now there's even a water-phase epoxy combination. It serves as either a coating or an adhesive. Before it sets, you can use water to wash it from brushes and tools, but after it sets, it's completely waterproof. Complete setting takes about 8 hours.

- **Superglues** are modern adhesives with amazing holding power, particularly suitable for bonding non-porous materials such as metals, glass, ceramics, porcelain, rubber and most plastics. Among them are the cyanoacrylates, urethanes and silicones. Most live up to the claims made for them provided they are used precisely according to the manufacturer's instructions. *Caution:* These superglues stick to anything including human skin. Take care to avoid getting any on your hands during use.

- **Mastic adhesives** are heavy-bodied pastes that are extremely tacky and fast-bonding. They are available in cartridge tubes for easy application with a caulking gun when you're installing wall panels, stair treads, metal thresholds, ceramic tiles, parquet flooring and other building materials. Specialized varieties are designed for masonry work such as brick and block laying, patching and repairing. Some are available in more economical five-gallon cans.

One manufacturer has a light colored mastic for adhering wall panels to studs or furring strips. After a bead of mastic ⅛ to ¼ inch wide is laid along the stud, it's best to delay hanging the panel for up to 15 minutes. Good bonds develop in 48 to 72 hours, but it takes 28 days for the mastic to reach full strength. It can even be applied to wet lumber.

Solvents are potentially a problem with many adhesives. Standard contact cement includes naphtha or toluol, for example. Toluene, acetone, and xylene are among other popular solvents. Such solvents give off flammable vapors at temperatures as low as 40°F. (4°C.) or even 15°F. (−18°C.) in the case of acetone. The National Safety Council says the vapors' main hazard sometimes comes from their "profound narcotic effect." However, the vapor can also build up until it's explosive.

Industry sources are saying that solvent adhesives are on the way out. You're well advised to pick water-base glues when you can. Solvents are less likely to be a problem and clean-up will be easier.

Keep cool for less money

■ IF YOU THOUGHT the *only* way to keep cooler in the summer was to buy a huge airconditioning system, think again! A smaller one may do just fine.

And if you thought being more comfortable costs an arm and a leg, think again! You might even get by with a simple fan that moves the air to cool you down.

A lot depends on where you live; a lot depends on how much you have to spend; and a lot depends on just how comfortable you want to be.

This article will give you some ideas to improve your home comfort. In some cases, you won't have to spend a cent, and where you do, we'll help you make some wise choices.

There are two things that make you uncomfortable in the summer—heat and humidity. Humidity is moisture in the form of microscopic droplets of water. You have some good choices to battle the heat and humidity by changing the moisture level or the air flow.

Room humidity and body humidity

Humid air is what makes you feel sticky. Your body, which cools itself by perspiration, can't evaporate water (sweat) from the skin's surface when humidity is high. The air is too full of moisture already to take on any more from your body.

Dry air can be just as uncomfortable, but if you can control humidity you have a cheap weapon against the heat in some parts of the country.

Cool appliances

Here are some of the options you have to make your home cool and comfortable.

Airconditioners both cool room air and act as dehumidifiers. They reduce humidity to a comfortable level by "drying" the air of humid, heat-holding water droplets. But an airconditioner is not your only choice.

Dehumidifiers (units that remove water only) can be used in special high-humidity places such as basements, laundry and bathroom areas where moisture is generated naturally from the ground or from washing or bathing.

Evaporator coolers can be used in the Southwest to pass hot room air over a small water reservoir to draw heat from the air and exhaust it in the form of heated water.

Fans (table, window, ceiling or attic) can circulate air, exhaust air, bring in cooler outside air (after the sun goes down), or just blow on you and help dry the sweat on your skin.

Economizers are great systems that take a message from an automatic control system and sense when outside air is cooler than inside air (usually in the evenings). They then use a system of sensors to open dampers on a vent to the outside to bring in free-cooling air. This can result in a tremendous savings in energy in parts of the country where it gets cool in the summer after sundown.

Set-up thermostats can be added to most forced-air systems so you can save a bundle on energy by raising temperatures at night (after you're asleep) or during the day when you're away from home. You can set these automatic systems to turn on just in advance of when you plan to return home so the house has already started cooling when you arrive.

Other cooling tips

In addition to high-tech equipment and automation to make you more comfortable, be sure you remember all the things you do in winter that help conserve energy—caulk around windows, wrap ductwork, increase overhead insulation (12 in. is standard now), close and cover windows on the sunny southern side of your house during the day but open them at night if it gets cool (your well-insulated house will retain heat unless you ventilate it), and set the thermostat up (a setting of 70° to 80° can cut energy use by 15%).

Choosing your airconditioner

For most efficient cooling, a room airconditioner must be suited to its load. Too small and it won't do the job; too large and it will fail to control humidity, and its compressor will run

ESTIMATING COOLING LOAD

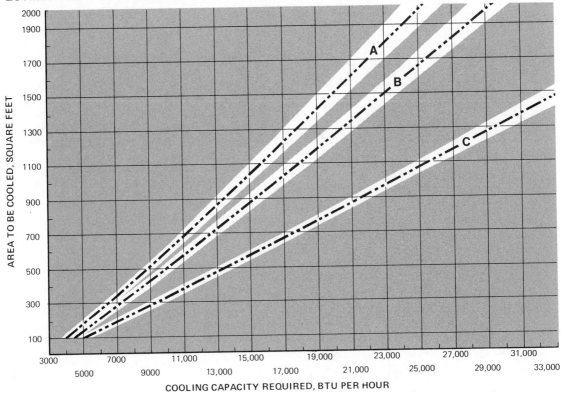

intermittently—while you will have paid more for the unneeded capacity. The Association of Home Appliance Manufacturers (AHAM) has a method to determine cooling load based on the graph above.

Determine the floor area to be cooled (in square feet) and then locate this figure on the left side of the graph.

Then move across to the intersection of lines A, B or C depending on what's above the space you want cooled. If the space above is occupied, use line A. If there is an attic with insulation on the floor, use line B. If the attic has no insulation, use line C.

From the intersection, move down (to the left) the appropriate line for more northern exposure or up the line (to the right) for more westerly exposure.

From this point read down to the bottom of the graph and note the BTU number for the cooling capacity required. This is a preliminary figure for the cooling load.

Now subtract 30 BTU per hour for each linear foot of wall separating the area to be cooled from other cooled rooms. If more than two people oc-

cupy the area, add 600 BTU per hour for each additional person; if only one person occupies the area, subtract 600 BTU per hours. Add 4000 BTU per hour if the area contains a kitchen.

Now locate your geographic area on the map and multiply your BTU-per-hour figure by the appropriate factor for the part of the country you live in. The resulting number is the cooling capacity you require. If, however, the room aircon-

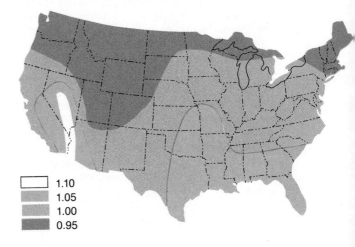

☐	1.10
▨	1.05
▧	1.00
▓	0.95

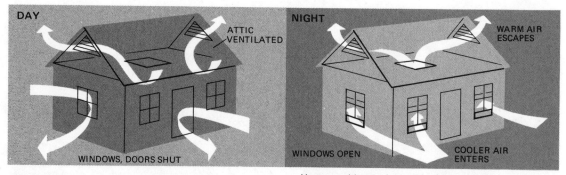

DAY

ATTIC VENTILATED

WINDOWS, DOORS SHUT

NIGHT

WARM AIR ESCAPES

WINDOWS OPEN

COOLER AIR ENTERS

ditioner is intended primarily for night use, reduce this amount by 30 percent.

Check the Energy Efficiency Ratio (EER) on the Federal Trade Commission's yellow Energy Guide label that must be on all room airconditioners. A room airconditioner's EER is found by dividing its electrical input in watts into its cooling capacity in BTU per hour. EERs between 5 and 7 are common for smaller units, but high-efficiency models with EERs of 11 and higher are also available, and usually cost more initially. From the cost of electricity in your area, and knowledge of your family's habits of cooling use, you can estimate how long a high-efficiency unit will take to repay its higher initial investment.

Locating your airconditioner

Install a room airconditioner on the north side of the house where it will be out of the sun as much as possible. If this can't be done, build a sun screen or plant a tree to shade the unit. Locate the airconditioner away from the clothes dryer vent—humid air from the clothes drying puts an unnecessary load on the a/c and lint could cause clogging.

Comfort without airconditioning

Houses without airconditioning can still be livable if closed up tightly when the outdoor air becomes warmer than indoor. Circulation to the attic should be prevented. At night, let cooler air enter through windows. Warmer air rises through to the attic and escapes out vents in the gables.

A hot attic radiates heat downward, and an inadequately ventilated attic can easily reach a temperature of 150°F. or higher. While insulation between attic floor joists cuts radiation, cooling the attic by improving its ventilation will also increase comfort in living areas. A powered ventilator (louver) governed by a thermostat is mounted as high on the roof as possible, and used with gable or soffit vents of adequate size. General practice calls for the effective area of these vents to equal 1/300 of the attic floor space.

Houses without airconditioning can still be livable if closed up tightly when outdoor air becomes warmer than indoor. Circulation to the attic should be prevented. At night, cooler air can be allowed to enter via windows. Warmer air rises through entrance to the attic and escapes out vents in the gables.

A hot attic radiates heat downward, and an inadequately ventilated attic can easily reach a temperature of 150° F. While insulation between attic-floor joists cuts radiation, cooling the attic by improving its ventilation will also increase comfort in living areas. A powered ventilator (louver) governed by a thermostat is mounted as high on the roof as possible, and used with gable or soffit vents of adequate size. General practice calls for net free area (effective area) of such vents to equal 1/300 of the attic floor space.

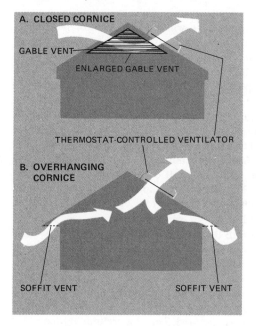

A. CLOSED CORNICE

GABLE VENT

ENLARGED GABLE VENT

THERMOSTAT-CONTROLLED VENTILATOR

B. OVERHANGING CORNICE

SOFFIT VENT

SOFFIT VENT

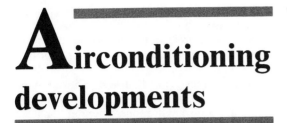Airconditioning developments

■ ROOM AIRCONDITIONERS were introduced to the home in 1929. In the 1970s, after some 40 years of development, product design and performance were at a standstill—some experts said there just wasn't much room for improvement.

So homeowners were faced with rather simple buying decisions—how much cooling for how much money. Only the quality of the product and the performance record of the manufacturer swayed many homeowners to buy one unit rather than another.

High-tech breakthroughs

Those are still valid buying criteria. But there are three breakthrough developments that are taking room airconditioning technology off its side track and putting it on the main line with other high-tech products.

The first big change came with application of an advanced-design rotary compressor room airconditioning—a change in the way units are made. This new design has gained dramatic acceptance for performance and price in the American market, successfully challenging the proven reciprocating design that was the industry standard. Seasonal Energy Efficiency Ratios (SEER) of these new rotary units are in the 10 to 15 range, as compared to the SEER of 6 or 7 of older reciprocating units. (SEER is a measure of how much energy is used to get a specific amount of cooling—a measure of performance. The higher the SEER the better; an acceptable rating is in the 7 to 9 range.)

The second important change is the application of sophisticated electronic circuitry and development of a new system theory where two or more room evaporator units are fed off a single outside condensing unit. We are changing the way we use room a/c units. It's the same modular concept used in automated offices where a main computer terminal operates multiple desktop computers.

Third, in the next three years, the concept of smart electronics will change the way we think about all home appliance products, including the room airconditioner.

The rotary compressor

The rotary compressor design has multiple value built in. First, it has fewer parts than the piston-type reciprocating compressor (51 compared to 128, and only three of these move). There are fewer things to fail. The economy of design results in a lighter weight, so it's easier to move and install. The lighter weight and smaller overall design means it can be shipped at lower cost. This results in better prices to consumers.

The rotary compressor uses a simple rotating motion of a crankshaft within a single compression cylinder instead of the back-and-forth reciprocating motion of pistons in cylinders.

The rotary's "roller" piston and the spring-loaded vane that rests against it divide the chamber into two volumes of continuously varying size. On one side of the vane, gas is pulled into the chamber, and on the other side the gas in the chamber is compressed and discharged. This means virtually all of the volume is used for

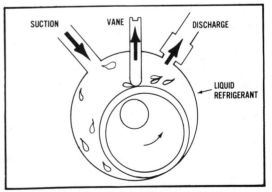

THE ROTOR TURNS on an eccentric shaft, drawing refrigerant gas in through the suction port then compresses it when the chamber gets smaller as the rotor turns in its orbital path. A moveable vane separates the high-pressure discharge side from the suction side.

nearly perfect design operating efficiency. It also means compact size and less weight—40 to 50 percent smaller than reciprocating compressors of the same capacity.

The rotary compressor has constant suction, with the suction port isolated from the discharge port by the vane and roller. This eliminates the need for a suction valve, a primary cause of compressor failure in reciprocating units.

There is no need to mount a rotating compressor on spring-mounted platforms as reciprocating units must be to absorb the back-and-forth vibration of the pistons.

Some manufacturers have built combination all-season units that function in a way similar to a heat pump. These use the rotary compressor in the same unit to power cooling in the summer and heating in the winter.

Electronics and system theory

Homeowners are getting more sophisticated household appliances. The key to it all is the electronic chip (IC) with its integrated circuits. Technology has found a way to put many electronic circuits on a "chip" of silicon small enough to be held by a tweezers—some small enough to pass through the eye of a needle. The introduction of high-power "smart chips" can now control the high current and voltages of appliances like room airconditioners directly. The electronic chip now used in airconditioner circuits is essentially the same technology we find in microcomputers.

With the development of the computer chip, we can do more things on a single electrical circuit. We can *program* the unit—tell it what to do at specific times. For example:

Setback/setup. The IC enables presetting temperatures so you can have the a/c unit off, or at a higher temperature, during the times your room is unoccupied. Then it automatically cools down to the temperature you want when you get home.

Staging. Some advanced controls can "stage" temperature changes so temperature will rise, or decrease, in orderly increments. For instance, you may want to start to sleep cool, but not sleep all night breathing cooled air. So you set the control to let the a/c raise the temperature slightly higher during the night, then drop again before you get up.

Balance control. An IC can strike a balance between the heat in the air and the moisture in the air—between heat and humidity. Dry air holds less heat than wet (humid) air. Sometimes, even though you have the temperature set at one place, you still need dehumidification—an IC

balance control will regulate humidity separately from temperature and at the same time.

Remote control. An IC will receive and process signals from remote, wall-mounted or hand-held control devices.

Split system. This IC-based innovation has enabled a breakthrough in design theory for room a/c units applications. The traditional single unit becomes part of a *system* that includes evaporator-only units located in different rooms of a house. These units are "split" by having a single compressor, located outside the building, circulating refrigerant to evaporator units located

NEW SPLIT-UNIT room airconditioners mounts the compressor outside with only a small hole cut for refrigerant and power lines.

CUT-AWAY VIEW

Compressor
Partition plate
Outdoor fan
Outdoor fan motor
Air discharge grille
Outdoor heat exchanger
Wall case
Room cabinet
Outdoor rear grille
Air-intake
Control panel
Indoor fan motor
Indoor fan
Air filter
Electric heater
Drain pan
Base pan
Electrical control box
Indoor heat exchanger

INSIDE, THE EVAPORATOR of a split a/c unit can be hung like a picture on any wall, even an inside wall between rooms with lines run in the walls.

ROOM-SIZE heat pumps provide heating and cooling comfort year round from the same unit. Common in motels, these units are becoming more popular in homes.

in each room where you want cooling. Not only does this let you locate the noisier compressor outside, the quieter evaporator unit can be hung on the wall like a picture—even on an inside wall between two rooms.

Smart technology

New in development is a whole new home wiring system called the "Smart House." Instead of previously conventional alternating current (ac) where the electrical current changes direction 60 times a second, there will be a direct current (dc) line that will provide power, communications and television capabilities over one-way dc wires wrapped inside a single cable.

The meaning of the "smart" technology for room a/c units is that you can now combine the improved controls you get with ICs with *thinking* options programmed into the system to cover more and more comfort and energy-conserving conditions.

Occupancy. For example, the "Smart" programmed room a/c will lower cooling to an approximate level, say within five degrees, but not cool it further until the room is occupied. Sensors tell the control system when someone has walked into the room, and the a/c is turned on. When everyone leaves the room, it will sense that and turn the a/c off—but only after a time to prevent cycling on and off in a room where you're watching TV, for example, and leave to get a snack during commercials.

Usage. Occupancy can be programmed for long periods of time and the individual room a/c units can be selectively set for operation. You can have your workshop cooled only on weekends, or the den or sewing room only when you need it.

The technology of the space shuttle missions has and is continuing to find its way into our homes—now through our room airconditioning units.

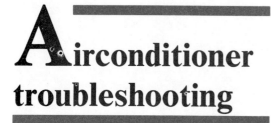

Airconditioner troubleshooting

■ IF YOU FIND after a winter's "hibernation" that your room airconditioner doesn't work as well as it did last summer, don't call for service right away. There are a number of checks you can make to determine what's wrong and pin-point the part or parts that need replacing. You'll be surprised at what you can save by doing your own appliance repair.

It may be that the air filter is simply dirty. A dirty filter restricts airflow over the cooling coil and cuts efficiency as much as 30 percent. Some models have a permanent-type germicidal filter made of spongy material that can be washed in soap and water, rinsed, squeezed dry and rein-

Noisy operation

POSSIBLE CAUSES	ACTION TO TAKE
1 Tubing vibration.	Reshape or bend tubing so there is no rubbing of tubing against metal.
2 Fan blade loose on shaft or bent.	Check to make sure that blade does not spin freely on motor shaft. Bend or straighten fan blades until the noise is minimal.
3 Fan motor loose on mounts.	Tighten fan motor mounts. Check motor alignment.
4 Loose parts.	Check installation for tightness, cover for tightness, and look over the entire unit for loose screws or washers.

Unit drips water

POSSIBLE CAUSES	ACTION TO TAKE
1 Cabinet not properly leveled.	Adjust unit so that it has a slight downward pitch toward outside end (Maximum pitch ¼ in.)
2 Condensate drain holes plugged.	Check and clean holes of any blockage.
3 Slinger-ring fan on condenser out of adjustment.	Check slinger-ring clearance from base pan. It should be 1/16 in. Too much clearance reduces water pickup.
4 Extreme humidity.	Sweating formations are normal under these conditions. Try to improve all seals and minimize window or door openings.

stalled. Others have fiberglass filters that should be replaced when laden with dust and lint.

The unit's inner compartment should also be cleaned. Although there are two types of chassis—one that slides out like a drawer and one that has to be totally removed from the window—both are cleaned the same way: Use a vacuum cleaner to blow dirt and lint off the condenser and evaporator. Then clean the compressor, fan motor and blades and tubing with a quickly evaporating solvent such as trichloroethylene, sold in hardware and paint stores.

When reinstalling a window unit, especially the chassis-type that does not slide out, be sure it is properly tilted for condensate flow and drain of water (usually ⅛ to ¼ in. low on the outside). Finally, make sure the unit is plugged in.

On older models, during the hottest days of summer, it's good practice to operate the airconditioner on Maximum or High Cool. At this setting, air is cooled, filtered, dehumidified and circulated at the highest rate. On average summer days and at night, switch the unit to Low Cool to reduce current draw and prevent possible icing up of the evaporator on cool nights. Newer models have automatic thermostat shut-off to eliminate manual switching and maintain a constant comfort level.

Unit will not run

POSSIBLE CAUSES	ACTION TO TAKE
1 Blown fuse or open circuit breaker.	Check voltage at wall receptacle with test lamp. If lamp doesn't light, replace fuse or reset circuit breaker. Make certain airconditioner is off.
2 Broken or loose wiring connection.	Check service cord at wall outlet and cord connections on control switch.
3 Defective thermostat.	Unplug unit. Turn thermostat to Cool position. Check for continuity (uninterrupted connection) across thermostat's terminals with a continuity tester, available at hardware stores. If no continuity exists, replace the thermostat.
4 Defective start capacitor.	Unplug unit. Remove start capacitor (the smaller of two capacitors located behind control panel). Replace with new capacitor of the same rating.

Fan runs, compressor does not

POSSIBLE CAUSES	ACTION TO TAKE
1 Defective thermostat.	Turn thermostat to High Cool, place jumper wire across thermostat terminals. If compressor comes on, replace thermostat.
2 Defective run capacitor.	Unplug unit. Remove run capacitor (the larger of two capacitors behind control panel) and replace it with new one of the same rating.
3 Overload switch open or defective.	Remove overload switch (may be attached to outside of compressor). Place continuity tester across overload terminals. There should be a reading if overload is at room temperature (70° F.). If no reading, replace overload.
4 Loose or broken wiring connections.	Check all wiring and terminals. Clean all rust and replace defective wiring and terminals.
5 Mechanical "stall" or defective compressor.	Temporarily hook up compressor directly to power line to see if it will run (try this only on 117-volt models, not on 220-volt types). Do this for just a few seconds. If compressor fails to start, a new compressor may be needed.

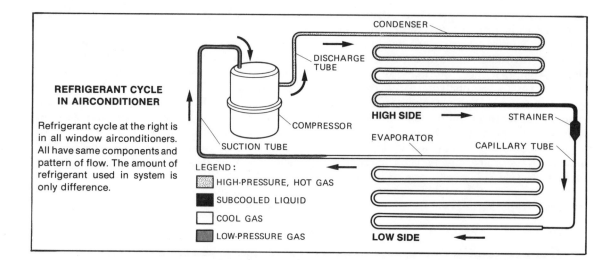

REFRIGERANT CYCLE IN AIRCONDITIONER

Refrigerant cycle at the right is in all window airconditioners. All have same components and pattern of flow. The amount of refrigerant used in system is only difference.

LEGEND:

- HIGH-PRESSURE, HOT GAS
- SUBCOOLED LIQUID
- COOL GAS
- LOW-PRESSURE GAS

Compressor runs, but fan does not

POSSIBLE CAUSES	ACTION TO TAKE
1 Defective fan switch.	Unplug unit. Place continuity test lamp across High, Medium and Low terminals on switch (refer to the manufacturer's schematic). If no reading is indicated at any or all terminals, replace switch.
2 Defective fan capacitor.	Unplug unit. Replace fan capacitor (usually common with run capacitor) with one of exactly the same rating.
3 Defective fan motor winding.	Unplug unit. Check each winding (High, Medium and Low) of fan motor with continuity test lamp. Refer to wiring diagram for proper connections or bridge tester across switch terminals and ground on motor housing. If no reading is indicated in any winding, replace fan motor.
4 Blower wheel binding.	Try to spin blower wheel. Failure of wheel to spin freely is a result of improper clearance. Adjust blower wheel on motor shaft or blower shroud surrounding the fan assembly.

Unit blows fuse or trips circuit breaker

POSSIBLE CAUSES	ACTION TO TAKE
1 Unit restarted too soon after running.	Allow three to five minutes for the system to balance (pressures to equalize) before turning the unit on again.
2 Circuit overloaded.	Place the airconditioner on a line by itself and check for proper fusing.
3 Stuck or defective compressor.	See the section "Fan runs, compressor does not."
4 Defective run capacitor.	Unplug the unit. Then replace the defective part with a new run capacitor which has exactly the same capacity rating.
5 Wiring shorted or grounded to frame.	Check all electrical connections to the compressor and behind the control panel. Connections should be tight and should not touch any metal parts of the airconditioner.

Unit short cycling

POSSIBLE CAUSES	ACTION TO TAKE
1 Thermostat short cycling.	Evaporator is either blocked or dirty and must be cleaned. Make sure that only the thermostat sensing bulb is touching the evaporator and is clamped tightly to it.
2 Defective condenser.	Check the fan operation. If the fan should become hot and stop, replace the motor. Check the blades for clearance.
3 Condenser dirty.	Blow out the condenser (using the blower of your vacuum cleaner) until light can be seen through the fins.
4 Defective overload.	If the compressor isn't overheated, and the overload is at room temperature, and no continuity is read across the overload terminals, replace the overload switch.
5 Unit restarted too soon after running.	Allow from three to five minutes for the system to restore its pressure balance; then try restarting the unit again.

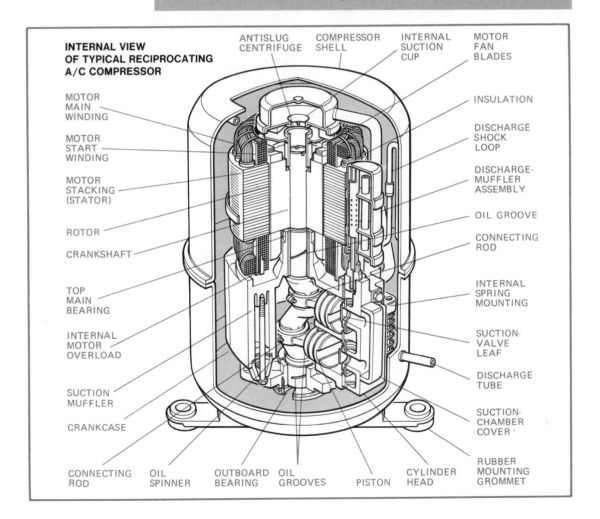

INTERNAL VIEW OF TYPICAL RECIPROCATING A/C COMPRESSOR

ANTISLUG CENTRIFUGE

COMPRESSOR SHELL

INTERNAL SUCTION CUP

MOTOR FAN BLADES

MOTOR MAIN WINDING

INSULATION

MOTOR START WINDING

DISCHARGE SHOCK LOOP

MOTOR STACKING (STATOR)

DISCHARGE-MUFFLER ASSEMBLY

ROTOR

OIL GROOVE

CRANKSHAFT

CONNECTING ROD

TOP MAIN BEARING

INTERNAL SPRING MOUNTING

INTERNAL MOTOR OVERLOAD

SUCTION-VALVE LEAF

SUCTION MUFFLER

DISCHARGE TUBE

CRANKCASE

SUCTION-CHAMBER COVER

RUBBER MOUNTING GROMMET

CONNECTING ROD

OIL SPINNER

OUTBOARD BEARING

OIL GROOVES

PISTON

CYLINDER HEAD

Unit not cooling

POSSIBLE CAUSES	ACTION TO TAKE
1 Thermostat set warm.	Turn thermostat to a higher setting.
2 Filter dirty.	Check filter for dirt accumulation. Light should be able to pass through it. Replace or wash filters according to brand.
3 Condenser dirty or restricting airflow.	Blow out condenser with vacuum cleaner and clean fins of all dirt buildup.
4 Compressor won't run.	See section "Fan runs, compressor does not."
5 Leaking seals.	Check all seals around window. Make sure windows are shut and that curtains or furniture don't block unit.
6 Undersized unit.	Make heat survey of room for correct B.T.U. size of unit. Check according to accompanying directions.
7 Refrigerant leak.	Check amperage (current draw) of unit while it runs (you can do this if you have an ammeter handy). Compare current reading to manufacturer's nameplate amperage rating to see if motor is drawing current properly. If current draw is below rated amperage and everything else checks okay, this may indicate a refrigerant leak. Test for leaks by rubbing soapy solution over outside of tubing and around joints. Watch for bubbles that show up leaks. If leaks are found, call serviceman to repair and recharge unit.

PROPER EXTENSION-CORD WIRE SIZES AND LENGTHS
(For use with 117-volt airconditioning units)

LENGTH OF CORD (in feet)	AMPERES REQUIRED (see nameplate on units)							
	6	8	10	12	14	16	18	20
				AWG Wire Size				
to 25	18	18	16	14	14	12	12	12
26-50	16	16	14	14	12	12	12	10
51-75	14	14	12	12	10	10	10	8
76-100	14	12	12	12	10	10	8	8

Evaporator frosts over

POSSIBLE CAUSES	ACTION TO TAKE
1 Restricted airflow over evaporator.	Check for dirty filter, blocked air passages, lint buildup on the blower wheel or blocked fins on the evaporator. Clean all items.
2 Outside temperature too low.	If temperature outside drops below 70°F., either turn unit off or set thermostat at Low Cool and fan at Low speed.
3 Thermostat too high or defective.	Lower setting of thermostat. If problem still exists, turn thermostat off and check for continuity between the terminals. If a reading exists, thermostat is defective and must be replaced.
4 Refrigerant leak or undercharge.	See section "Unit not cooling" above.
5 Low fan speed.	Check fan for higher speed, binding at housing, loose blade on shaft or defective motor. Correct or replace motor.

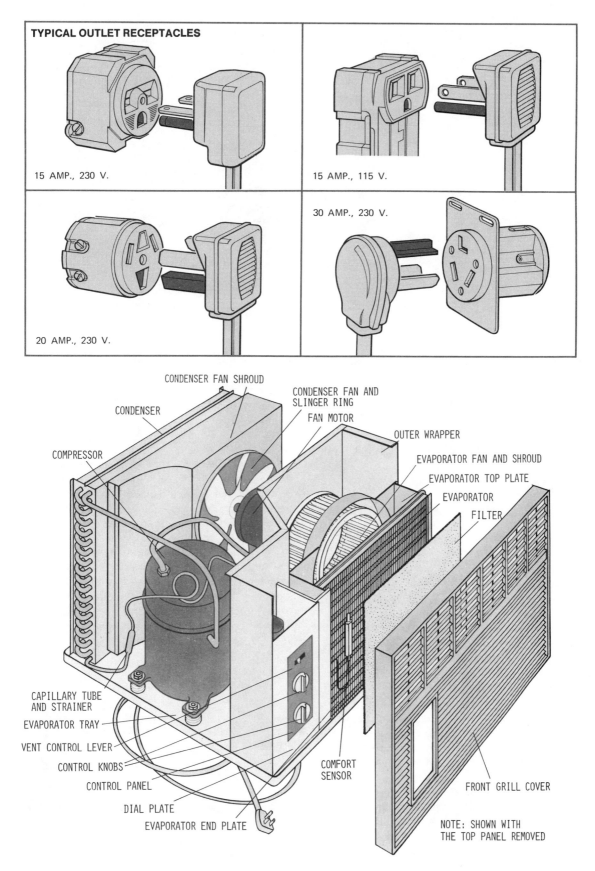

TYPICAL OUTLET RECEPTACLES

15 AMP., 230 V.

15 AMP., 115 V.

20 AMP., 230 V.

30 AMP., 230 V.

CONDENSER FAN SHROUD

CONDENSER FAN AND SLINGER RING

FAN MOTOR

CONDENSER

OUTER WRAPPER

COMPRESSOR

EVAPORATOR FAN AND SHROUD

EVAPORATOR TOP PLATE

EVAPORATOR

FILTER

CAPILLARY TUBE AND STRAINER

EVAPORATOR TRAY

VENT CONTROL LEVER

CONTROL KNOBS

CONTROL PANEL

DIAL PLATE

EVAPORATOR END PLATE

COMFORT SENSOR

FRONT GRILL COVER

NOTE: SHOWN WITH THE TOP PANEL REMOVED

Angles: how to measure and cut them

■ A LINE STRAIGHT across a board forms a 90° angle to the edge. This 90° angle is the essence of construction. If you can mark and cut squarely the length, width and thickness of just one board on a true 90° angle, you can do it for all other angles and for all size boards.

Joinery, the process of connecting two or more pieces of wood, created the need to accurately measure angles. Mitered joints made it necessary for the carpenter to measure angles precisely. The common mitered joint is 90°, with each half piece cut at 45°. When mitering, the smallest error in measuring or marking, even a fraction of a degree, can leave a gap between the two pieces of wood. That results in a less attractive-looking and much weaker joint.

Precision in measuring angles is not new. Angles for the stones in Egyptian pyramids, built 5000 years ago, have the same tolerances as today's prescription eyeglasses. A look in today's hardware stores and mail order tool catalogs reveals many ingenious instruments for measuring angles. Many are amazingly similar to tools used to measure and mark material for Pharaohs' tombs.

Basic tools

Basic tools used for measuring angles include the try square, combination square, bevel square, protractor and framing square (also called carpenter's, rafter or steel square). Many hardware stores carry other tools that combine several instruments.

Try squares measure the basic angle—90°. The term *try square* comes from its use in testing, or trying, the accuracy of a cut. It is used to mark, then test, 90° angles only. It consists of two parts—stock (or handle) and the blade (or tongue); both parts are securely joined together at right angles. The stock is thicker than the

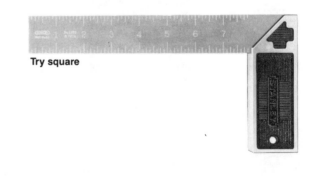

Try square

blade so it wil butt against the edge of the material and let the blade rest on top. Woodworking try squares come in varying sizes, from short, 3-in. blades to long, 18-in. blades. The most frequently used, handier sizes, fall within 6 to 12 in.

Combination squares can be used to mark both 90° and 45° angles. You don't have to purchase individual measuring tools, such as outside try square, inside try square, marking square, depth gauge or miter square. The combination square frequently has a cast iron head with either a 12, 18, or 24-in. blade that slides through the head. The blade can be fixed at any point by a knurled nut. The head is designed to test, or mark, a 90° angle on one side and a 45° angle on the other. Most combination squares have bubble levels, and some have a small, pointed scratch awl for marking.

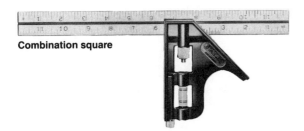

Combination square

Bevel squares are used to lay out and mark projects such as corner braces, dovetails, or side rails for chairs. It is actually an adjustable try square. Blade sizes range from 6 to 12 in. or more. Because it is adjustable, it is excellent for getting into places where angles are difficult to measure. Use a protractor to accurately adjust the angle. You can also use a framing square to adjust the angle of a bevel square for most common angle cuts.

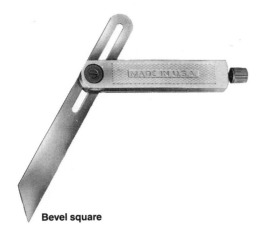

Bevel square

Framing squares are also called carpenter's squares or rafter squares and they are a variation of a large try square. Both legs of the framing square are usually ⅛ in. thick. The wider, longer part is called the blade; the shorter, narrower part the tongue. Printed on the framing square are various measurements and factors that are used in measuring the angle and length of roof rafters, staircases and similar angled projects.

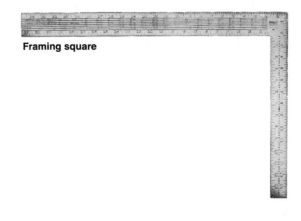

Framing square

Miter boxes are designed to assist in angle cutting with hand tools. The wood is placed in the miter box and held against its fence. Boxes have limits to the size of the wood that can be used. Inexpensive boxes have fixed saw guide slots; angle cuts are usually only at 45° and 90°. Better miter boxes adjust saw blades to any angle. Quality miter boxes have guides to hold the saw firmly and clamps to steady the wood.

Miter box

Miter gauges are found on most table and bench saws (and a variation on some circular saws) and are marked to turn the stock or tilt the blade to a specific angle.

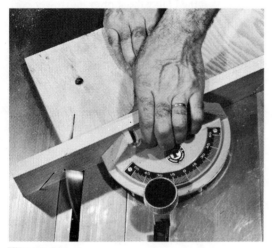

Miter gauge

Square corners—as easy as 3-4-5

You can lay out or test the squareness of right angles of huge corner room partitions as easy as 3-4-5. A triangle with measurements of 4 units (feet, inches, yards or whatever) along one base and 3 units along the other must measure 5 units across the diagonal between the ends of these lines if the angle where the two base lines meet is 90°.

For example, to see if a bookcase unit is square, measure 4 ft. along the base of the unit and 3 ft. up the side. The distance between your mark on the base at 4 ft. and your mark on the side at 3 ft. will be exactly 5 ft. if the unit is square with a true 90° angle.

If you want to draw an accurate 90° line up a wall from the floor, you can measure 4 ft. out from the point where you want the line. Then take a 5-ft. piece of mason's twine (or anything that won't stretch) and mark an arc on the wall roughly over the spot. Then move your twine back to the starting point and scribe another arc on the wall 3 ft. up from the floor. A line drawn from start of your base line to the point where the two arcs cross will be a true 90° to the floor. You can increase the accuracy of this line by drawing a 10-ft. arc 8 ft. out across the floor and a 6-ft. arc up the wall from your starting point. The laws of mathematics don't care what the units are as long as they are in the same proportions.

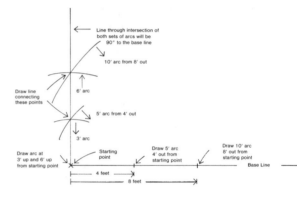

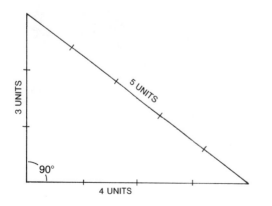

Squaring large rectangles

When measuring large rectangular pieces like tall bookcases or window frames, it is easy to test if all four corners are square. The distance between the top left corner and the bottom right corner must be the same as the distance between the top right corner and the bottom left corner if the unit is square and all angles the proper 90°. If the unit is skewed—tilted to one side—the distances between one set of the two opposite corners will be longer than the other.

Measuring other angles

Any carpentry project, from building a house to building a coffee table, is going to run into other angles besides the 90° and 45°. This is where measuring gets tricky.

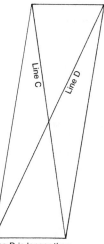

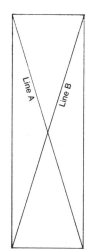

Line D is longer than line C.

Line A is same length as line B. Unit is square

(top of the wall units) to the ridge. *Hip rafters* extend diagonally from the ridge to an outside corner of two walls. *Valley rafters* are similar, but these extend from the ridge to an inside corner where two walls meet. A *jack rafter* is anything that doesn't go all the way from the top of the wall plate to the ridge.

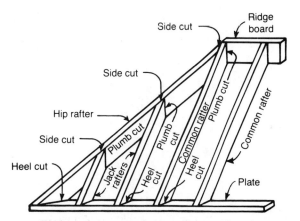

Rafters are a good example of the many different kinds of angles, but angles are not limited to work on roofs; you will find these same kind of angles and compound angles in any project with three or more sides or in picnic table legs and wall decorations, to name just a few.

The most helpful tool for measuring and drawing these angles is the framing square. Since this tool was designed to be used in making rafter cuts, we'll explain its use there, although the same principles will apply if you are cutting the legs of a picnic table or building an octagon-shaped coffee table.

Fitting pieces together on the roof involves at least three different angles. The *plumb cut* is the angle of the common rafter at the ridge board. This angle must be straight up and down (or plumb) so both sides of the roof fit together without gaps and at the same angle. On the other end of the common rafter is the *heel cut,* where the rafter sits on the plate at the top of the wall unit. Jack rafters (either hip or valley jacks) will have to have a compound angle at one end, the *plumb cut* to be at the same slope as the common rafters and a *side cut* to meet the hip or valley rafter running on an angle to the corner.

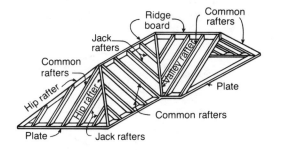

Look at a roof frame to see the kinds of shapes involved. The *ridge board* is the horizontal piece used to connect the upper ends of the rafters on one side to the rafters on the opposite side. A *common rafter* extends diagonally from the plate

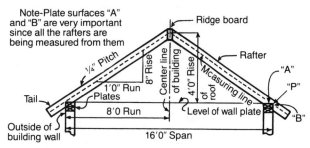

There are a few more things about roof terminology you should know. The *span* is the distance between the wall plates. The *run* is measured from a plumb line from the ridge to the wall. This is usually one-half the span distance, but roofs or

other projects do not have to have symmetrical slopes on both sides of the high point. The *rise* is the distance from the top of the wall plates to the top of the ridge.

Now let's see how a framing square can help you measure and cut these angles with craftsman precision.

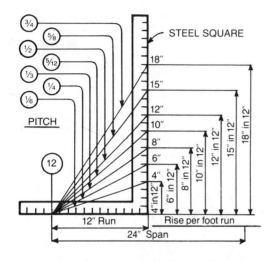

The basic 3-4-5 technique mentioned earlier is based on the principle that the line completing a right triangle (where one angle is a true 90°) has a fixed relationship to the length of each of the triangle's other two sides. If you measure 4 in. out the tongue of a framing square and 3 in. up the blade, the line between these two points will be 5 in. long. This represents a rise of 3 in., a run of 4 in. and let's assume a span of 8 in. The rafter cut to fit this roof would have to be 5 in. long to reach the ridge 4 in. away from the walls. For convenience, however, the framing square uses a fixed point of 12 in. along one base to determine the angle and length of the other two sides. In our example, then, the framing square measurements

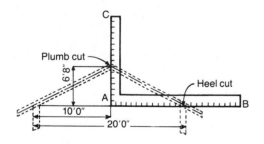

instead of 3-4-5 would be 12-16-20 (each measurement is multiplied by 4).

If you could put a huge framing square on

your roof with the 90° angle plumb with the center of the ridge, the measurement along the base would be the run and the measurement up the tongue would be the rise. The angle of the plumb cut at the ridge and the heel cut at the top plate of the wall could be drawn on the rafter, then taken away to cut. Framing squares of this size are, however, hard to find and would be impractical to use.

The makers of framing squares make it easy for you to get the same angle measurements with smaller squares. A rise of 6 ft. 8 in. (80 in.) in a run of 10 ft. is the same as a rise of 8 in. every foot.

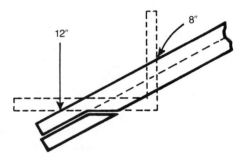

The *heel cut* can be made by placing the 12-in. mark on the blade on the edge of the rafter board, the moving the tongue so the 8-in. mark meets the same edge. A line drawn along the blade will be the correct angle to sit on top of the wall plate. At the other end of the board, with the framing square located the same way, a line down the tongue will be at the correct angle for the *plumb cut* to meet the ridge board.

A framing square will have printed or etched on it factors you can use to multiply the length of the run to determine exactly the length of the board you'll need for the rafter. The height of the rise will always make the rafter longer than the run.

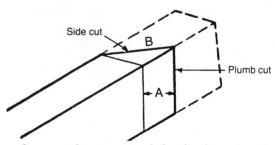

Once you have mastered the simple angles of the heel cut and plumb cut, the compound angles of the side cuts in hip, valley or jack rafters should go easy. Several scales on the framing square tell you what measurement along the blade of the square to place on the piece of wood (with 12 in. on the tongue) to draw the correct angle for a side cut.

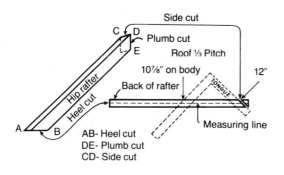

For example, for our rise of 8 in. every foot of run, the scale on the framing square indicates 10⅞ in. Place the 12-in. mark on the tongue along the inside edge of the board with the tongue extending to the plumb cut. Then twist the square until the 10⅞ in. mark on the blade is along the same edge of the board. The line drawn along the tongue will give you the correct side angle cut for this hip or valley rafter. Different scales are used for jack rafters.

Using the framing square for polygon angles

A polygon is any shape with three or more sides. A three-sided polygon is a triangle; four-sided polygons are squares or rectangles; eight-sided polygons are octagons; and the pentagon is nothing more than a five-sided polygon.

This table gives the tongue and blade measurements for common-size polygons. If you are going to build an octagonal (8-sided) aquarium coffee table and wanted 8 angled pieces of plywood cut to form the base, you would measure 12 in. out from the place where you want the point of the piece, then measure 4³¹⁄₃₂ in. up at a right angle from this point. A diagonal line connecting these two points will give you the proper angle for one cut of your piece. Measure 4³¹⁄₃₂ in. at a right angle down from point 12 in. out from the tip and you have the mark to draw the diagonal line for the other cut. Extend both diagonal lines until the distance between them is the measurement you want for the outside edge of each leg of the octagon. Eight pieces cut this same way should fit together into a tight-fitting octagon with no unsightly gaps or weak joints to glue.

Other uses for the framing square

Framing squares have many other uses, not the least of which is laying out the proper angles, rise and tread for stairs. Most manufacturers include a well-illustrated booklet with framing squares that gives you step-by-step instructions for all of its many uses. If there is not one with the square you plan to buy, look for a square that has one. Another word of caution: Carpenter's squares and some try squares look like framing squares but do not have the essential measurement factors for length of rafters and side-cut angles printed or embossed on the blade. A good framing square will probably cost a little more than a carpenter's square of comparable quality, but the increased utility in measuring and cutting angles for any project you do is well worth the small extra cost.

POLYGONS AND THEIR MITERS
USE FIGURES ON SQUARE

	Tongue	Blade		Tongue	Blade
3 Sides	12 in.	20 7/8 in.	10 Sides	12 in.	3 7/8 in.
4 Sides	12 in.	12 in.	11 Sides	12 in.	3 17/32 in.
5 Sides	12 in.	8 25/32 in.	12 Sides	12 in.	3 7/32 in.
6 Sides	12 in.	6 15/16 in.	14 Sides	12 in.	2 3/4 in.
7 Sides	12 in.	5 25/32 in.	16 Sides	12 in.	2 13/32 in.
8 Sides	12 in.	4 31/32 in.	18 Sides	12 in.	2 1/8 in.
9 Sides	12 in.	4 3/8 in.	20 Sides	12 in.	1 29/32 in.

As Shown Below

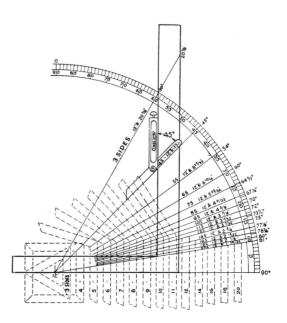

Cutting compound angles

COMPOUND CUTS are made with both the blade and miter gauge tilted the required degrees. The blade guard has been removed for picture clarity.

■ GETTING THE FOUR CORNERS of a "hopper"-style picture frame to fit is fairly easy, but determining the degree of bevel for a simple four-piece box with sides that slope, say 35°, can be puzzling. For example, the butt joints of the box appear to be 90°, when viewed from the top, but when they're viewed in a true plane, you'll find the "square" edges are less than 90°— actually 70½°. That's the tricky part of compound angles: The bevel does not show in a plan drawing, and even when you study the completed job, the angles are not what they seem.

Compound angles are required when sawing the parts of any pyramidal shape of four, six or eight sides, and are made with the blade (or table, as the case may be) tilted to cut a bevel and the miter gauge swung to cut a miter. Thus both the miter and the bevel are cut in one operation.

The chart on the next page takes all the guesswork out of setting your saw to cut a number of common compound angles. It gives the required tilt for the saw blade and the swing (tilt) of the miter gauge in degrees.

The fastest and most economical way to saw parts for sloping box or flared frame is from a long board which has been prebeveled along both edges. This is called strip cutting. The miter gauge is left at the same setting and the board is flopped after each cut. When the parts are individually cut from scrap, the miter gauge is turned around and used backward for the second cut so wide side of work is always against the miter-gauge facing.

The upper drawings on this page show four standard miter-gauge positions for strip cutting—A and B for cutting miter joints, C and D for butt joints. Here the blade tilts to the right.

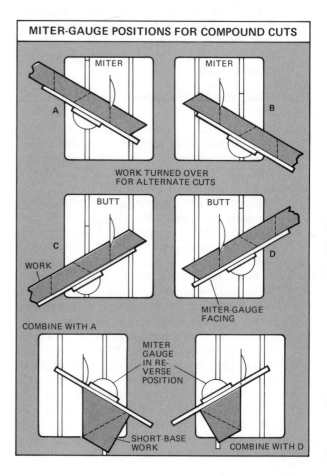

MITER-GAUGE POSITIONS FOR COMPOUND CUTS

The two sets of positions are pairs worked by shifting the miter gauge from one table groove to the other. Prebeveling the edges is done so the top and bottom edges of the pieces will be on a flat plane when assembled. If the box sides slope 35°, for example, the top and bottom edges are beveled 35°.

You can use any of the four miter-gauge positions shown when the work is not prebeveled. However, only two of these positions can be used when the work is prebeveled and the job calls for mitered joints at all four corners, as the bevel must bear against the miter gauge with the sharp corner facing up. When a peak is to be formed like the roof of a birdhouse, and cut from individual prebeveled pieces, the long side of the work must be held against the miter-gauge facing for both cuts; the bevel must face up for both cuts.

In the case of rough work, compound joints are simply butted and nailed or, for greater strength, glued and nailed. However, in finer work, splines are used. These are thin strips of wood cut to fit saw kerfs made in mating members.

WEAR SAFETY GOGGLES

WHEN PARTS ARE cut individually from separate pieces, the first cut is made with the work held in the position shown above.

TO MAKE the second cut, the miter gauge is turned around and used backward. The same miter-gauge setting is used.

SAW-TILT AND MITER-GAUGE SETTINGS FOR COMPOUND ANGLES

FRONT VIEW — ANGLE

4 SIDES, BUTT JOINTS

4 SIDES, MITER JOINTS

6 SIDES, MITER JOINTS

8 SIDES, MITER JOINTS

WORK ANGLE	SAW TILT	MITER GAUGE	SAW TILT	MITER GAUGE	SAW TILT	MITER GAUGE	SAW TILT	MITER GAUGE
5°	1/2	85	44-3/4	85	29-3/4	87-1/2	22-1/4	88
10°	1-1/2	80-1/4	44-1/4	80-1/2	29-1/2	84-1/2	22	86
15°	3-3/4	75-1/2	43-1/4	75-1/2	29	81-3/4	21-1/2	84
20°	6-1/4	71	42	71	28-1/4	79	21	82
25°	10	67	40	67	27-1/4	76-1/2	20-1/4	80
30°	14-1/2	63-1/2	37-3/4	61-1/2	26	74	19-1/4	78-1/4
35°	19-1/2	60-1/4	35-1/4	60-1/4	24-1/2	71-3/4	18-1/4	76-3/4
40°	24-1/2	57-1/4	32-3/4	57-1/4	22-3/4	69-3/4	17	75
45°	30	54-3/4	30	54-3/4	21	67-3/4	15-3/4	73-3/4
50°	36	52-1/2	27	52-1/2	19	66-1/4	14-1/4	72-1/2
55°	42	50-3/4	24	50-3/4	16-3/4	64-3/4	12-3/4	71-1/4
60°	48	49	21	49	14-1/2	63-1/2	11	70-1/4

Figures are in degrees and are for direct setting to tilt scale and miter-gauge scale provided tilt starts at 0° and miter gauge at 90° in the normal position.

American antiques

■ EXPERTS IN ANTIQUES agree that a question most often asked is, "How can you tell if it's old?" The experts use common sense and a keen eye for distinguishing incorrect elements. These instincts are gained from years of study. There are some specific qualities you can look for in judging if an item is old and possibly antique.

Woods. You should first know the kinds of woods used in making furniture in earlier times. Certain woods are indigenous only to the United States, and some even more specifically to only certain parts of this country. Some woods are no longer in great supply; therefore, they were often not used for furniture after a certain date. Some of these are identified later in the description of specific styles and periods of American furniture.

Style. Styles of construction are age indicators. These include, for example, beaded molding on drawer fronts and dovetailing used to construct drawers. Stylistic elements such as the American eagle and the flag are also age indicators. These symbols were used on furniture and other decorative accessories at the turn of the 19th century to signify the founding of our country. You should be skeptical about any piece with these decorative elements that is said to be from the period around the American Revolution. Noting any incongruities in style will help to date a piece.

Tools. An understanding of what tools were used in making old pieces of furniture can help you tell their age. Before the early part of the 19th century, planing or dressing wood was done by hand. Marks made by hand tools look like ripples in a brook. When there are no signs that hand planes were used and the piece is said to be from an early period, be suspicious. After 1850 few hand planes were used. The circular saw was introduced into general use after 1840. If you see circular saw marks on a piece that is said to be from the 18th century, you should be wary.

Hardware: Hand-wrought nails were used until almost the turn of the 19th century. After this time, cut nails made by machine were introduced. Screws can also be a clue in determining the age of an antique. Handmade screws, uneven and irregular in shape, were used (although not as much as nails) until the early part of the 19th century. Hardware such as brass and iron handles and decorative elements such as glass inserts and ormolu mounts also give indications of age. Some of the hardware characteristic of specific periods of American furniture are illustrated later in this article.

Additional clues. All wood shrinks across the grain. As moisture evaporates from the wood, its shape changes. It contracts and pulls itself toward the center. Expect signs of shrinkage in genuine old pieces. Look for cracks in the wood or loose-fitting joints.

Holes from worms or other vermin may signal age for some antique pieces. You must be wary, however, of holes that are too precise or too regular.

Paint surfaces can also suggest age. Of course, no acrylic or oil-based paints were used on early American furniture. There should be some markings on old paint indicating normal wear through time and use. Often a top coat of varnish was applied to protect the thin milk paint and the wood. Even through this varnish, there should be signs of aging on the paint such as nicks, scrapes or scratches. There may also be what is called crazing or crackling (cracking) of the finish, indicating that the wood under the paint has shrunk.

The term 'antique'

Before 1967 and for the purposes of importing, the United States Customs Service ruled that any piece made before 1830 was technically considered an antique and could enter the United States without duty payment. The choice of the early 19th-century date reflected the transition from hand to machine manufacture and the emergence of the Industrial Revolution. For many people, however, any item at least 100 years old is considered an antique. And even today, the government concurs in that date. There are also those items that we remember seeing and using earlier in our lives. Many of these, such as player pianos and roll-top desks, are in both short supply and great demand, so they have become collectibles and are loosely referred to as antiques by some.

Is it valuable?

You can make both aesthetic and value judgments about individual antique pieces. Some have historical importance because they are connected to some famous person or event in the past. The monetary value of these items may be affected by their history, while the aesthetic value will probably not.

The size of an object affects its value now as much as it affected whether it was fashionable when it was made. For example, during the early 19th century delicate narrow spindle legs on chairs and tables were in vogue. They were also more expensive. Later, into the middle of the 19th century, larger and more bulbous legs and feet were in favor.

Today, a slant-front desk in a highly figured tiger maple is far more desirable than just a maple desk. So the medium of the object also affects its desirability and, in this case, its value. The tiger maple desk is not commonly found, so rarity, measured by the supply and demand of the marketplace, can also be a consideration in the value of antiques.

The quality of workmanship and the skill in creating a finished product are also important in establishing the worth and beauty of an object. Patina is the soft mellow look achieved through age, use, air and climate; it gives an antique its charm, individualism and character. It is also another way to determine its value. The skinning of a piece during refinishing to remove the original color, line and age lowers the value in both an aesthetic and monetary sense.

Repairs and restorations

Repairs. If a piece of furniture is maintained in its original condition, its ability to retain and eventually increase in value is far greater than a piece that has been altered. In some cases, however, repairs to old things are necessary and even recommended. Repairs, especially those that let you continue using the piece, are acceptable. These should be done the same way the original maker would have done them.

Restorations. Restorations are repairs with new parts added. Again, restoring a piece can increase its life and usefulness if the restoration uses the techniques of the original maker.

Reproductions. A reproduction is a replica, a copy of the original made to look like the original. Even though its original conception was old, a reproduction will not have either the aesthetic or the monetary value of the original. A new piece made totally from old wood is not a repair and is not a restoration. It is a new piece made from old wood. This is known in the antiques world as a *marriage*.

Styles and periods of American furniture

Furniture specialists have designated seven major periods of American furniture. These begin with the discovery of the United States and continue to the turn of the 20th century. Although these styles closely followed English traditions, each period has individual features distinguishing it from its European counterpart and reflecting a specific period in history.

Pilgrim period (1460–1700). The first of these, the Pilgrim or Jacobean period, is derived almost exclusively from the Elizabethan or Jacobean English style. The primary woods used at this time were oak and pine. Ornamentation was done by turnings (on a lathe), joining by mortise and tenon, carving and ebonizing (painting the turnings black). Other decorative features were applied bosses, spindles, geometric panels, ball turnings and massive baluster supports.

William and Mary period (1700–1725). The William and Mary period also closely followed the English tradition. It favored dark woods, especially walnut, with additional application of burlwood and veneering. The favored stylistic elements were trumpet-shaped spiral legs, ball feet and teardrop drawer pulls. Applied and carved decorative scroll motifs were in C and S shapes. Stylization was angular.

in this period. Brass decorations were usually ornate and intricately carved. Regional schools of furniture expanded in the United States during this period.

Queen Anne period (1720–1750). During the Queen Anne period, stylization was curvilinear. The most distinguishing characteristic introduced during this time was the cabriole leg. This was a graceful, curving leg usually terminating in a pad-shaped foot known as the Queen Anne foot. The woods were primarily walnut, mahogany, cherry and maple. Attention to wood graining and veneering was added for heightened interest. Key plates and drawer mounts or pulls were bat-wing-shaped. In the early 18th century regional centers of cabinet making with their own highly individualized elements of style were developing in Connecticut, Massachusetts, Rhode Island, New York and Philadelphia. The influence of the Orient was also felt during this period. Furniture in imitation of Oriental lacquer wood known as *japanned* wood made its debut in the United States.

Chippendale period (1750–1790). Mahogany was the most frequently used wood in the Chippendale period. This style was based on Thomas Chippendale's book, *The Gentlemen & Cabinet-Maker's Directory,* first published in England in 1754. The furniture of the period is characterized by Gothic, Rococo or Chinese design elements. Decorative motifs used were scrolls, finials, carved shells and acanthus leaves. The Chinese influence was evident in fretwork carving. Legs were either cabriole with Rococo carving at the knees or square and blocked in the Chinese manner. The ball and claw foot was most often seen

Federal period (1785–1820). Two important source books influenced the Federal style. The first, published in England in 1788 by George Hepplewhite, was *The Cabinet Maker's and Upholsterer's Guide.* The second was Thomas Sheraton's *The Cabinet Maker and Upholsterer's Drawing Book,* published in parts between 1791 and 1794. Both were guides for what was considered tasteful and fashionable at the time. The primary wood was mahogany, lightened by using wood graining. Satinwood inlaid motifs and shallow carving were also used. The Federal style is best characterized by a light, graceful classical form having straight, slim, tapering legs, turned reeded legs or splayed French feet. Tambour doors were used, as were oval-shaped brass mounts. Decorative motifs included the use of drapery, swags, urns, medallions, sheaves of wheat, the Prince of Wales feather, the eagle and the shield.

Empire period (1810-1840). During the Empire period, mahogany, cherry and maple were the dominant woods, all having a reddish stain. There was an emphasis on classical motifs with heavy, ornate carving in naturalistic forms. Feet were often in the form of large animals' legs. The paws were decorated with carved leaves and scrolls. Sometimes claw feet and brackets were carved to resemble winged creatures. Marble used as tabletops and ormolu complemented busily carved friezes and pilasters. Ogee columns, used to accentuate basic lines, flanked chests of drawers and cupboards. The ponderous size of these pieces meant construction of three or four pedestal bases as table supports. Other decorative elements were the lyre, eagle, leaves, grain and fruit forms.

Victorian period (1840-1900). From the middle of the 19th century to its close, there was a return of interest to earlier styles of furniture. The repetition of decorative ornamentation and stylization happened over a long period of time. The Victorian era has often been called a "century of revivals." Here are some of those revivals:

Gothic revival (1840-1865). Inspired by medieval designs, furniture makers used trefoils, intri-

cate designs and pointed arches. Walnut, mahogany and rosewood were the preferred woods.

Elizabethan revival (1840-1870). This revival saw the reproduction of machine lathing, making it possible to give posts, rails, legs and spindles spool, ball or spiral-turned decorative features. Mass-produced furniture in less expensive woods such as maple, cherry and birch appeared for the first time. Also at this time, cottage furniture (the first low-cost mass-produced furniture) was produced in suites, especially for the bedroom. These suites were either painted or stained mahogany.

Rococo revival (1845-1870). This period is most widely known because of the development of a new process of working with woods called *lamination.* The wood, either rosewood or walnut, was cut into thin sheets, heated, then bent into a desired shape. Entire suites of furniture, most often for the parlor, were produced. Ornate decorative embellishments were shaped like shells, fruits, flowers and birds. Marble was also used to complement the tops of tables and chests.

Renaissance revival (1850-1875). Mahogany, rosewood, satinwood and inlay were often used

on Renaissance revival furniture. Turned legs and carved and applied ornaments in Renaissance designs were popular, as were incised lines carved into decorative patterns and then gilded.

Egyptian revival (1850–1890). Decorative motifs such as winged figures, animal forelegs, hairy paw feet, sphinxes and numerous combinations of animal and human forms were used.

Eastlake style (1870–1890). Derived from a book by Charles L. Eastlake, *Hints on Household*

Taste: in Furniture, Upholstery and Other Details, the furniture is rectilinear and has shallow carving, framed paneling and false front drawers.

Styles of furniture

Colonial and Early American furniture. The terms *Colonial* and *Early American* are colloquial expressions handed down from generation to generation and not actual period designations. The dictionary defines both Colonial and Early American as relating directly to the period of American history around the American revolution. But the terms often mean anything that looks old and is made of pine.

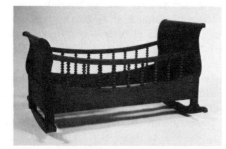

Country style. Essentially the recognized periods describe highly styled American furniture. Throughout the settlement of the United States and until the introduction of the Empire style in the early 1800s, the principal design sources in this country were derived from England. It was in the 19th century that decorations from France and other countries became important influences.

As the early joiners and cabinet makers became acclimated to their new world, they built on their early training with adaptations and modifications and made them distinctly their own and American.

During this same time period, there were small groups and even individual craftsmen who were producing pieces of country furniture in a less sophisticated style. Country furniture was not made by highly skilled technical craftsmen, nor was it made in city cabinet shops.

Painted style. "Early American" most probably brings to mind the honey-colored pine furniture shown in stores today as the "Early American" look. These pieces, however, do not give an accurate picture of the color of the furnishings of our ancestors. Tables, chairs, clocks, beds, chests, cupboards and even boxes and picture frames were colored with paint.

Pine was the most commonly used wood. It was often covered with a milk-based paint of red, blue, white or green as a preservative. Different combinations of these colors were also used. The paint was often applied in patterns and designs, sometimes extremely lavish. Painting cheaper woods was also done to make them look fancier or to create intriguing designs. Sometimes the stylization of these pieces mimicked the more formal and fancier furniture. Other times the surface was painted in a grained or marbleized pattern. The result was most often an individualized and personalized creation.

Unfortunately, the true extent of painted furniture will never be known. Very few examples have survived. Over the years, many pieces were damaged or the paint was worn beyond recognition just in normal use. Many other pieces had to survive periods when stripping was considered more desirable.

The craftsmen who applied the basic paint were followed in time by the artisans who enhanced the finished product by applying their creative skills. It was the American artisans of the 19th century who made the strongest statement with paint decorations.

The brush was the basic tool used in decorating with paint. Amateurs and professionals alike, however, used a wide variety of other implements—feathers, corn cobs, combs, sponges, crinkly paper, potatoes, hands, arms, fingers, fists and even candle smoke, which produced a soft, hazy finish. Brushes were largely replaced in the 19th century by graining combs made in England. These combs were usually metal and came in all widths, thicknesses and teeth-spacing. Some combs were made of leather for more flexi-

bility, and some even of ivory. Still later, to speed the work and to satisfy the greater demand for painted furniture, large rollers made of metal, wood, linoleum or cut and etched rubber were used for printing distinctive patterns. Hand-held rollers were also made for the home handyman. The results were a bit crude, but a piece treated this way could cheer up otherwise drab surroundings with its colorful decoration.

Painting began with the application of a suitable base coat, usually a light color. After this was thoroughly dry, a contrasting graining color—a darker glaze in a fast drying paint—was applied. This sometimes included a combination of various paints with a touch of vinegar or beer, depending on the desired effect. This graining coat was allowed to set just enough so it would not spread out when combed or become too dry for graining. When it reached this stage, the craftsmen, using one or more tools, completed the pattern.

Do-it-yourself antique reproductions

There are dozens of individual projects in this set of the *Popular Mechanics Do-It-Yourself Encyclopedia* to help you acquire or develop skills in reproducing replicas of American antiques. You'll find four of these projects on the following pages here in Volume 1. Other projects are in the section on **Furniture Projects** in Volume 11 and **Cabinets** in Volume 4. Models of Colonial or Early American designs are found in many other sections throughout the 27 volumes. Help on duplicating an antique's finish is yours in the section on **Finishing** in Volume 10.

BIBLIOGRAPHY

Owning a library or having access to a good collection of books about antiques is a prerequisite for gaining additional knowledge. It will help lay a stronger foundation upon which to build. Reading about antiques will not, however, take the place of actually handling and looking at them.

Alexander, John D., Jr. *Make a Chair from a Tree: An Introduction to Working Green Wood.* Newton, Conn.: The Taunton Press, 1978.

Andrews, Ruth, editor. *How to Know American Folk Art.* New York: E.P. Dutton & Co., 1977.

Bishop, Robert. *American Folk Sculpture.* New York: E.P. Dutton & Co., 1974.

Bishop, Robert. *How to Know American Antique Furniture.* New York: E.P. Dutton & Co., 1973.

Christensen, Edwin O. *the Index of American Design.* New York: The Macmillan Company, 1958.

Coffin, Margaret. *The History and Folklore of*

American Country Tinware 1700-1900. Camden, N.J.: Thomas Nelson & Son, 1968.

Comstock, Helen. *American Furniture.* New York: The Viking Press, 1962.

Fales, Dean A., Jr. *American Painted Furniture 1660-1880.* New York: E.P. Dutton & Co. 1972.

Hayward, Dean A., Jr. *Colonial Lighting.* Boston: Little Brown, 1927.

Jacobs, Carl. *Guide to American Pewter.* New York: McBride, 1957.

Kauffman, Henry. *Early American Ironware, Cast and Wrought.* New York: C. E. Tuttle, 1966.

Ketchum, William C., Jr. *A Treasury of American Bottles.* Indianapolis: Bobbs-Merrill, 1975.

Ketchum, William C., Jr. *The Pottery and Porcelain Collector's Handbook.* New York: Funk & Wagnalls, 1971.

Kettell, Russell Hawes. *The Pine Furniture of New England.* New York: Dover Publications, 1956.

Kovel, Ralph and Terry. *American Country Furniture.* New York: Crown Publishers, 1965.

Lipman, Jean. *The Flowering of American Folk Art 1776-1876.* New York: Viking Press, 1974.

Lockwood, Luke Vincent. *Colonial Furniture in America, Volumes I & II.* New York: Charles Scribner's Sons, 1951.

Marsh, Moreton. *The Easy Expert in American Antiques.* Philadelphia: J.B. Lippincott Company, 1978.

McClinton, Katharine Morrison. *Collecting American 19th Century Silver.* New York: Bonanza Books, 1968.

Nutting, Wallace. *Furniture Treasury, Volumes I, II & III.* New York: The MacMillan Company, 1971.

Shea, John. *Antique Country Furniture of North America and Details of Its Construction.* New York: Van Nostrand Reinholt, 1980.

Smith, Nancy A. *Old Furniture: Understanding the Craftsman's Art.* Indianapolis: Bobbs-Merrill, 1975.

Build an old-time icebox

LID OF ICEBOX opens to reveal plastic-lined mixing compartment. Adjustable, recessed shelf (lower left) allows flexible storage.

■ OLD-TIME ICEBOXES, once a necessity, are now expensive collector's items. These plans incorporate many of the details used in turn-of-the-century ice chests in a handsome bar and storage cabinet. Like all 11 models shown in Sears' 1902 catalog, this icebox features frame-and-panel construction, brass hardware and casters. This slightly scaled-down version has a hinged lid that opens to reveal a mixing compartment lined with plastic laminate.

Materials note

The solid oak used in the icebox shown came dressed to 13/16 in. If you choose stock of different thickness or assemble it with different joints, alter the dimensions to compensate for the changes.

Frame assembly

Rip front frame rails and stiles (A,B,C,D and E) to the specified width. Then cut each part to length. Cut the mortises and tenons with a table saw, shaper, router or by hand. To ensure the frame fits together with tight glue lines, cut or sand $\frac{1}{32}$ in. off the end of each tenon. Seal the end grain on the three rails (C,D and E) and the center stile (B) with a 1:1 mixture of water and white glue. Apply the runny mixture to the tenon ends and shoulders. Let it dry about 15 minutes. Then apply full-strength glue to the tenon at one end of the center rail (D) and join it with the mortise of the center stile (B). Fit a scrap block with a mortise cut into it over the unjoined end of D to protect it, then clamp the parts. Check for

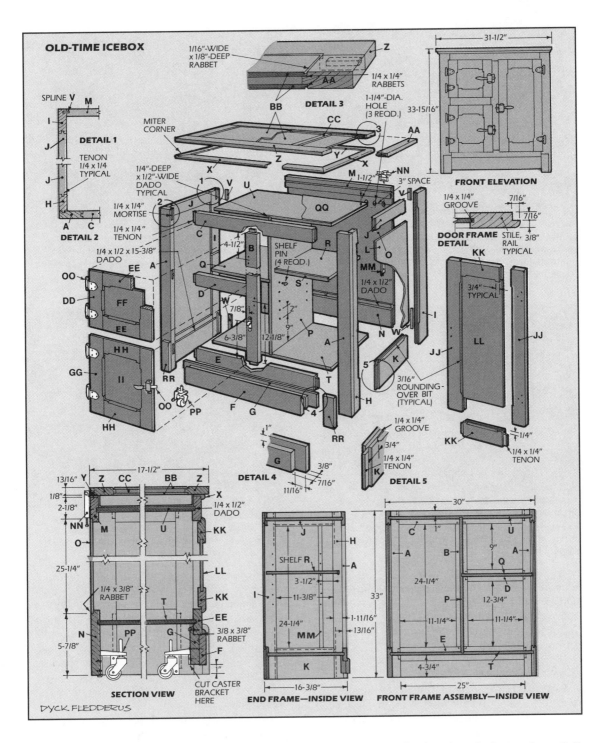

OLD-TIME ICEBOX

DYCK FLEDDERUS

squareness and let the glue set. Join the upper and lower rails (C and E) to the center stile. Then add the outer stiles (A).

Cut stiles (H and I) and rails (J and K) for the end frames. The front stiles (H) must have a ¼ x ¼-in. tongue milled into the front edge. Cut tenons in the end of the rails and cut grooves ¼

in. wide and ¼ in. deep into the inner edges of all end frame parts. The rear stiles are rabbeted to receive the back. Also cut mortises for the splines in these pieces. Cut end panels (L) from ¼-in. plywood with veneer that matches the solid stock. Dry-assemble the end frames without the panels and round over the inside edges with a ³⁄₁₆-in.-rad.

GLUING THE OUTER STILES completes assembly of the front frame. Use protective glue blocks to cushion stile edges from clamp jaws. Check the frame for squareness.

PANELS FOR CABINET ENDS fit into grooves cut into inner edges of rails and stiles. Check to make sure the panels slide in easily before joining the end frames with glue.

GROOVE THE INSIDE FACES of the cabinet's front frame to accept the inner compartment parts. Use a router with a straight cutter. Guide it on edge of straight board.

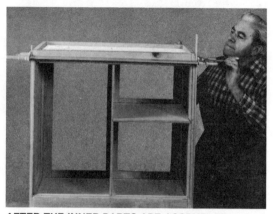

AFTER THE INNER PARTS ARE ASSEMBLED and glued into front frame and ends, add the back rails. Clamp them as shown above. Splines will be driven into the mortises.

rounding-over bit. Stop the cuts at a uniform distance (¾ in.) from each corner. Finish-sand all end parts before gluing assembly.

Follow the same gluing procedures as described for the front frame.

Making the compartments

Parts for the inner compartments of the icebox (P,Q,R,T and U) are cut from ½-in. fir plywood. Face the front of the adjustable shelf (R) with solid edging (S). Bore ¼-in.-dia. holes ⁵⁄₁₆ in. deep for adjustable shelf pins in the divider. Prepare a solid oak strip (MM) and fasten it to the inside of the large compartment end since the ¼-in. panel is too thin for the shelf pin.

The divider (H), bottom (T) and top (U) must all have dadoes ½ in. wide by ¼ in. deep. Cut a panel for the back (O) from ½-in. plywood and

the upper and lower back rails (M and N) from solid stock. Rabbet the back rails to accept the back panel. Cut grooves in the ends of the rails so they can be joined to the end frames with spline (V and W). Also cut the dummy drip pan door (F and G) and leg blocks (RR). Groove the inner faces of all frame parts and cut dadoes.

Assembly

Join the assembled cabinet ends to the front frame, clamp and let the glue set. Slide the bottom, top, divider and fixed shelf into what, at this point, is a three-sided box. Then, join the upper and lower back rails to the cabinet. Attach the back panel with ½-in. No. 4 flathead screws driven into the rabbets and divider. Attach the drip door assembly by screwing the ends of the backer to the back of the face frame stiles. Install

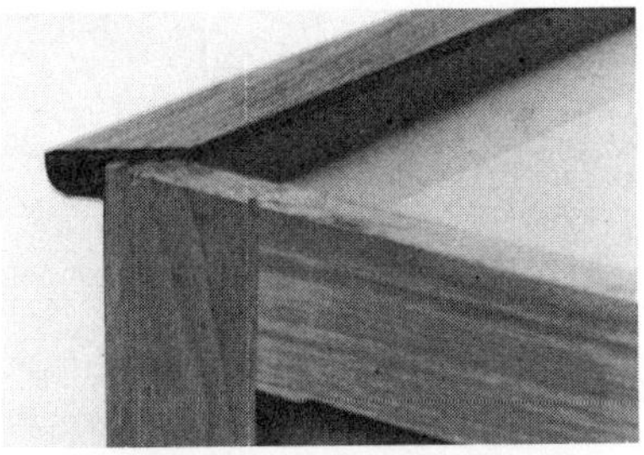

J-MOLDING, made up from solid stock that's rabbetted and rounded over, is applied to the mixing compartment's edges after lamination. Miter front corners, butt rear joints.

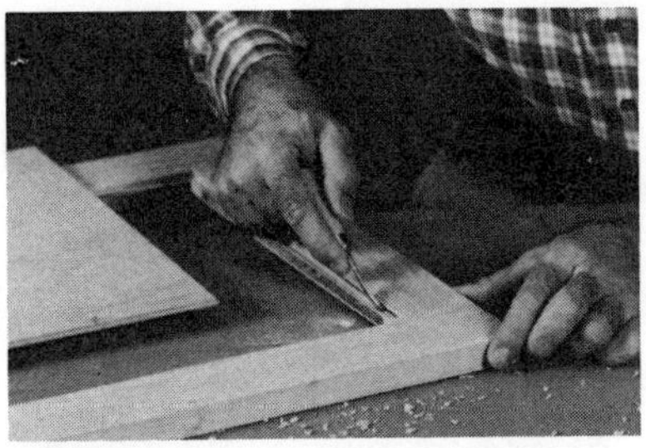

SINCE THE TOP FRAME is rabbetted with a router after being glued, round corners must be squared with a chisel before the plywood insert can be installed.

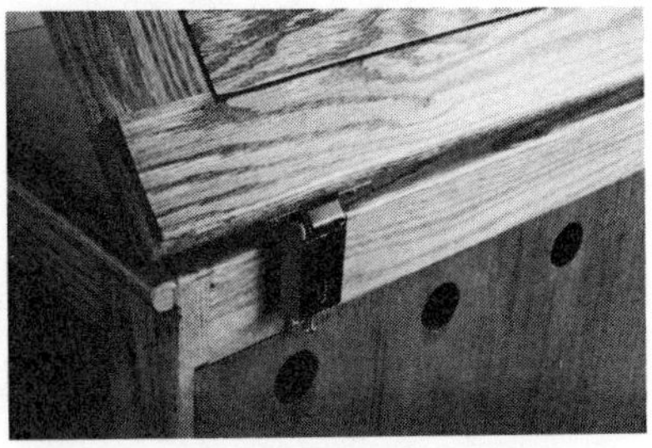

THE LID IS ATTACHED with spring-loaded hinges that can be adjusted to compensate for its weight. Turning the screw clockwise increases tension that holds the lid open.

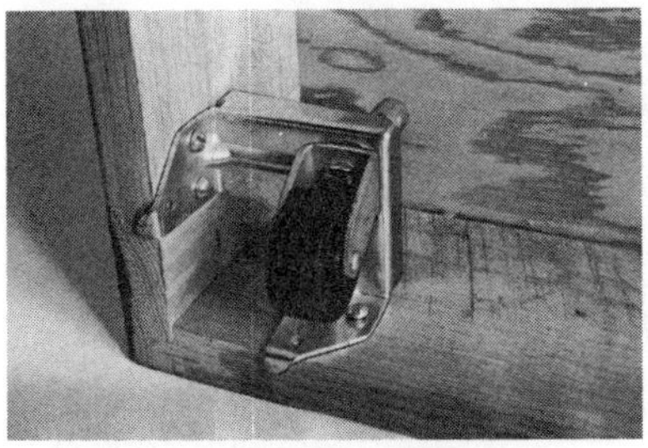

CONCEALED SWIVEL CASTERS have mounting brackets that attach to corners of the base.

MATERIALS LIST
OLD-TIME ICEBOX

Key	No.	Size and description (use)
A	2	13/16 x 2½ x 33″ oak (front stile)
B	1	13/16 x 2½ x 24¾″ oak (center stile)
C	1	13/16 x 2½ x 25½″ oak (front top rail)
D	1	13/16 x 2½ x 11¾″ oak (center rail)
E	1	13/16 x 2½ x 25½″ oak (drip pan door)
F	1	13/16 x 3½ x 25″ oak (drip pan door)
G	1	¾ x 3½ x 28⅜″ scrap (drip pan door backer)
H	2	13/16 x 1 15/16 x 33″ oak (front end stile)
I	2	13/16 x 2½ x 33″ oak (rear end stile)
J	2	13/16 x 2½ x 11⅞″ oak (end top rail)
K	2	13/16 x 6¼ 11⅞″ oak (end bottom rail)
L	2	¼ x 11 13/16 x 24 11/16″ oak veneer plywood (end panel)
M	1	13/16 x 2½ x 28⅜″ oak (rear top rail)
N	1	13/16 x 6¼ x 28⅜″ oak (rear bottom rail)
O	1	¼ x 25 x 29⅛″ fir plywood (back)
P	1	½ x 15⅜ x 27⅜″ fir plywood (divider)
Q	1	½ x 14 7/16 x 15⅜″ fir plywood (fixed shelf)
R	1	½ x 12½ x 13 ⅞″ fir plywood (adjustable shelf)
S	1	¼ x ¾ x 12½″ oak (shelf edging)
T	1	½ x 15⅜ x 28⅞″ fir plywood (bottom)
U	1	½ x 15⅜ x 28⅞″ fir plywood (top)
V	2	¼ x ½ x 2½ plywood scrap (spline)
W	2	¼ x ½ x 6¼″ plywood scrap (spline)
X	1	⅜ x 1 5/16 x 72″ oak (J-molding, rabbeted and shaped)
Y	1	⅛ x ⅞ x 29″ oak (trim)
Z	2	13/16 x 2½ x 31½″ oak (lid frame front and rear)
AA	2	13/16 x 2½ x 13″ oak (lid frame end)
BB	2	¼ x 13 x 27″ oak veneer plywood (lid insert)
CC	2	5/16 x ½ x 12½″ oak (lid stiffener)
DD	2	13/16 x 2½ x 9¾″ oak (top door stile)
EE	2	13/16 x 2½ x 7½″ oak (top door rail)
FF	1	¼ x 7 11/16 x 5 3/16″ oak veneer plywood (top door panel)
GG	2	13/16 x 2½ x 13½″ oak (bottom door stile)
HH	2	13/16 x 2½ x 7½″ oak (bottom door rail)
II	1	¼ x 7 11/16 x 8 15/16″ oak veneer plywood (bottom door panel)
JJ	2	13/16 x 2½ x 25″ oak (large door stile)
KK	2	13/16 x 2½ x 7½″ oak (large door rail)
LL	1	¼ x 7 11/16 x 20 7/16″ oak veneer plywood (large door panel)
MM	1	5/16 x ¾ x 24¼″ oak (adjustable shelf strip)
NN	2	Brass adjustable tension hinge
OO	set	Brass hardware including door hinges and latches
PP	4	Concealed swivel casters
QQ	6 sq. ft.	Plastic laminate
RR	2	13/16 x 2¼ x 5″ oak (foot)

Misc.: ⅝-in. No. 4 flathead screws, ¾-in. No. 8 roundhead screws, white carpenter's glue; contact cement; pigmented paste filler; sanding sealer or thinned shellac, semigloss lacquer; furniture rubbing compound.

the casters (PP). Caster brackets on the front pair must be cut.

To line the mixing compartment, first cut large bottom piece of laminate (QQ) to size and attach it with contact cement. Then cut narrow strips for the sides and attach them. The J-molding (X) is attached around the top edges of the mixing compartment. Join the front corners of the J-molding with 45° miters; butt the rear joints.

Top lid and doors

The top lid is of frame construction with a hollow center section. Cut solid stock for the rails and stiles (Z and AA) and prepare the mortises and tenons. Rabbet the inner edges of the frame after the pieces are joined. Use a chisel to square round corners left by the router bit. Glue the ends of the two stiffeners (CC) and fit them into the frame. Rabbet edges of the lid panels with kerfs 1/32 in. deep and 1/16 in. wide.

Construct the doors by using the same procedure used for the cabinet ends. After assembly, door front edges are shaped with a ⅜-in. rounding-over bit, and rabbets are cut in the back. Fasten the lid with tension hinges (NN) and attach doors with brass hardware (OO).

Once assembly is complete, remove the hardware. Fill the pores with paste filler and follow with two coats of sanding sealer and two coats of semigloss lacquer.

Antique mirrors you can copy

■ THE MIRRORS shown here were popular in the late 18th century and throughout the 19th. All three are in great demand at antique shops these days. However, they are becoming more difficult to get. These mirrors duplicate the original antiques.

Pine dressing mirror

Designed for use on a table or chest of drawers, this attractive dressing mirror is mounted atop a three-drawer cabinet. It's made entirely of pine to look authentic.

Start by cutting the base cabinet pieces as shown. Notice the cabinet's sides receive rabbets along the back and bottom edges. The cabinet's top and bottom pieces are rabbeted along the back edge. Take the time to sand all pieces thoroughly before assembly. This way, the cabinet will require only light sanding after assembly.

The cabinet's designed so you don't nail through the top or sides. All visible nailing is done through the cabinet's bottom and back surfaces. First, glue and screw the cleats to the cabinet's sides and partitions. Be sure to keep the cleats ½ in. back from the front edge to allow the drawers to close. Next, attach the partitions and the sides to the cabinet top's underside by screwing through the cleats. Finally, glue and nail the cabinet's bottom in place.

Cut lengths of ¾ x ¾-in. vinyl corner molding for drawer slides. If you can find rounded corner molding, plane the two outside surfaces flat before using it. Secure the slides in the cabinet with one ⅝-in. brad at each end. Next, cut all the drawer pieces according to the materials list. To avoid the cleats, the two smaller drawers' sides are narrower than the center drawer's.

Dry-assemble the drawers to be sure they fit smoothly into the cabinet. Make any adjustments before gluing and final assembly. With the cabinet assembled and the drawers fitting properly, glue and nail the cabinet's back in place using ⅝-in. brads.

Cut the pieces needed for the mirror frame, supports and braces. Before assembling the frame, cut rabbets into the frame's pieces to hold the mirror and hardboard back. Shape the front edges of the frame and all four corners of the two support pieces with a ¼-in. rounding-over bit.

Next, cut the bottom edges of the supports and braces at a 6° angle. Attach the braces to the supports using No. 8 roundhead screws as shown. Use a doweling jig to bore each brace's bottom for accepting two ⅜-in.-dia. dowels. Also, bore a ¼-in.-dia. hole through each support for installing the mirror adjusting knobs.

Before assembling the mirror's frame, bore a ⁵⁄₁₆-in.-dia. hole in each side piece for installing Teenuts. Since the Teenuts are installed backward from their designed use, bore two ¹⁄₁₆-in.-dia. holes in each Teenut as shown. Tap the Teenuts into the frame's sides, and then drive in two ⅝-in. wire nails to secure each one. Glue and nail the frame together with 1¾-in., 17-ga. wire nails at the corners. Clamp the frame square until the glue dries.

Before proceeding any further, use your lathe to turn the mirror adjusting knobs, drawer pulls and the cabinet feet. After turning the adjusting knobs, counterbore both ends of each knob as shown. Then, bore a ¼-in.-dia. through hole in each knob for installing a ¼-in.-dia. x 2½-in. stovebolt. Place a hexnut inside each knob and tighten the bolt to draw the nut flush with the knob. Fill the outside counterbores with wood filler to conceal the bolt heads.

Assemble the support members and the frame by screwing the mirror adjusting knobs through the supports and into the Teenuts in the frame's sides.

Now you're ready to join the mirror frame and supports with the base cabinet. Stand the frame

MATERIALS LIST
PINE DRESSING MIRROR

Key	No.	Size and description (use)
A	1	¾ x 8 x 28″ pine (cabinet top)
B	1	¾ x 8 x 27¼″ pine (cabinet bottom)
C	2	¾ x 8 x 4¼″ pine (cabinet sides)
D	2	¾ x 3½ x 7⅞″ pine (partitions)
E	4	½ x ¾ x 7⅜″ pine (cleats)
E1	11	1¼″ No. 8 flathead screws
E2	8	1″ No. 8 flathead screws
F	4	⅜ x 2⅞ x 7½″ pine (drawer sides)
G	2	⅜ x 2½ x 5″ pine (drawer back)
H	2	¾ x 4 x 6½″ pine (drawer front)
I	2	⅛ x 5¼ x 7⅜″ hardboard (drawer bottom)
J	2	⅜ x 3¼ x 7½″ pine (drawer side)
K	1	⅜ x 2⅞ x 11¾″ pine (drawer back)
L	1	¾ x 4 x 13½″ pine (drawer front)
M	1	⅛ x 7⅜ x 12″ hardboard (drawer bottom)
N	6	¾ x ¾ x 7½″ vinyl corner molding (drawer slide)
O	4	1¾″-dia. x 2⅛″ pine (feet)
P	3	1″-dia. x 1″ pine (drawer pull)
Q	2	1 x 1³⁄₁₆ x 20½″ pine (support)
Q1	2	1″ No. 8 roundhead screws
Q2	2	1½″ No. 8 roundhead screws
R	2	¾ x 2½ x 5½″ pine (braces)
R1	4	⅜″-dia. x 1½″ pine dowels
S	2	1⅜ x 1½″-dia. pine (mirror adjusting knobs)
T	2	¼″-dia. x 2½″ flathead stovebolts with nuts
U	4	¼″-dia. flat washers
V	2	¼″-dia. Teenuts
W	2	1 x 1³⁄₁₆ x 17¾″ pine (frame sides)
X	2	1 x 1³⁄₁₆ x 21⅞″ pine (frame top and bottom)
Y	1	⅛ x 16 x 20″ mirror
Z	1	⅛ x 16 x 20″ hardboard (mirror back)
Z1	1	⅛ x 4⅜ x 27⅜″ hardboard (cabinet back)

Misc.: Carpenter's glue, 8d finishing nails, 1¾″ 17-ga. wire brads, 220-grit sandpaper, ⅝″ 16-ga. wire nails, polyurethane varnish.

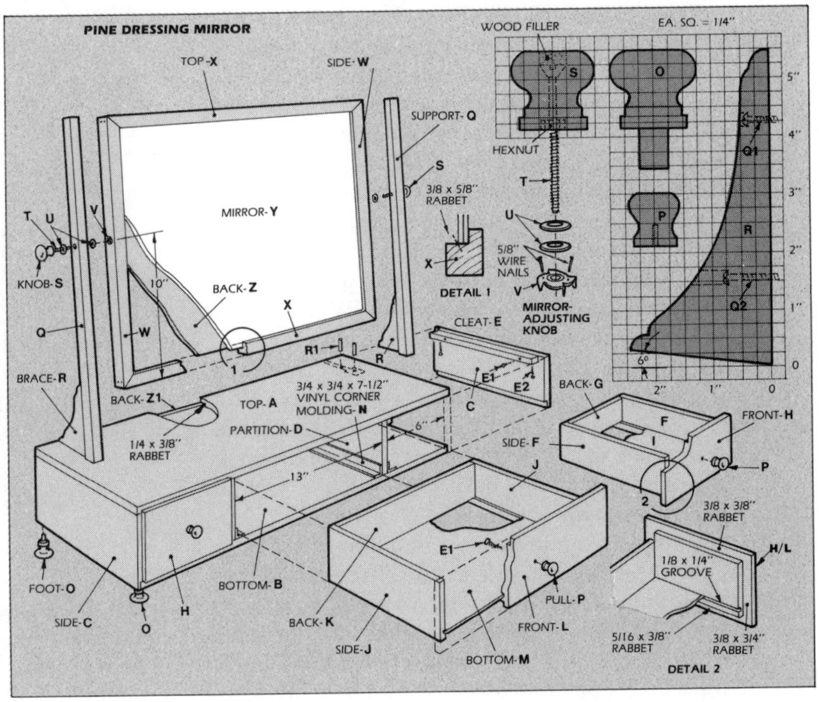

and support members centered on the base cabinet's top. Position the braces ¼ in. from the cabinet's back edge. Outline the two brace locations lightly with a pencil on the cabinet top.

Remove the frame and insert dowel centers into the holes previously bored in the braces' bottoms. Then, reposition the frame according to the pencil lines on the cabinet. Push down on the braces so the dowel centers transfer the dowel locations onto the cabinet's top. Bore ⅜-in.-dia. x ½-in.-deep holes into the top at these locations. Glue and insert the dowels into the braces, and then glue the frame and support assembly to the cabinet's top. Clamp and let dry. Attach the feet and drawer knobs to complete the assembly.

Chippendale looking glass

This wall-mounted mirror is made entirely of rich, ribbon-stripe mahogany; ¾-in. stock is used for the frame, ¼-in. mahogany-veneer plywood for the decorative scrolls.

Begin by cutting the mitered frame pieces to size. The frame's corners are joined using spline-reinforced miter joints. Splines produce tight, strong joints and ensure flush surface alignment. Use a table saw tenoning jig to cut ⅛-in.-wide spline grooves in the frame's miters.

Next, cut ⅛-in.-thick solid mahogany splines to fit the spline grooves. Be sure the grain runs across the spline's width to prevent splitting. Each spline has an inside corner cutout. Install the splines so this cutout will fit flush with the frame's inside corners.

Assemble the frame by first gluing the splines into the grooves and then clamping the frame square. Let the frame dry, then sand it.

Turn the frame face down on the workbench and rout a ¼-in.-deep x ⅜-in. rabbet into the back inside edge. This recess holds the mirror and the hardboard back.

Next, using a ½-in.-dia. straight bit, rout the eight circular notches into the frame's back for holding the hardboard back's tabs.

Set up the table saw with a ¼-in.-wide dado head to groove the frame's edges to hold the decorative scrolls. Cut the grooves ¼ in. deep along the length of the frame's top and bottom and partially up the frame's sides, as shown. Next, cut the ¼-in. mahogany-veneer plywood scrolls using a band saw, jigsaw or sabre saw. Use a smooth-cutting 24-tpi saw blade for a cut that requires little or no sanding. Notice the scroll's corners are mitered to allow the scrolls to abut tightly. Dry fit all scrolls before final positioning and gluing.

Since mahogany is an open-grain wood, you must fill the grain before applying the finish. To save a finishing step, mix the red mahogany stain with a natural wood filler. You can stain and fill the wood's grain in one step.

Brush the stain/filler mix liberally into the wood's grain. Let the filler dull over (about 20 minutes), then wipe off the excess with a coarse rag, such as burlap or terry cloth. Wipe against the grain, rubbing the filler into the wood's pores. Be sure to remove all excess filler from the wood's surface before it dries or you'll have a lot of sanding to do. Allow the filler to dry overnight, then sand lightly with 220-grit abrasive paper. Brush off the sanding dust, wipe with a tack cloth and follow with two coats of clear finish.

Complete the project by installing the mirror after the finish has dried. Attach the hardboard back to the frame with one ½-in. No. 6 flathead screw in each of the back's eight circular tabs. Then, insert two No. 16 screw eyes in the frame's top as shown to anchor the picture-hanging wire.

Cherry dressing mirror

The cherry dressing mirror is similar in design and construction to the three-drawer pine mirror. Often listed in antique books as a drawing glass, this late 19th-century piece is designed for use on a table or chest of drawers.

Start by cutting all the pieces to the sizes shown. Solid cherry hardwood is used through-

out. Before assembling the mirror's frame, rabbet the frame's pieces to hold the mirror and hardboard back. Also, shape the frame's two front edges and all four sides of both vertical supports with a ¼-in. rounding-over bit. The decorative scroll, feet and brace pieces are all shaped on a band saw, jigsaw or sabre saw. Use a lathe to turn the finials and the mirror adjusting knobs.

Next, cut the mortises in the feet using a router or shaper fitted with a ¼-in.-dia. straight bit. Make several passes, increasing the cutter's depth on each pass, until you reach a ¾-in.-deep mortise. You could also form the mortises by boring a

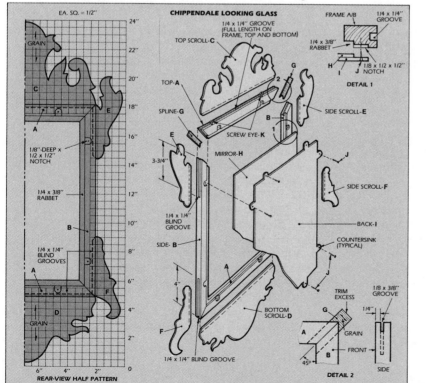

MATERIALS LIST		
CHIPPENDALE LOOKING GLASS		
Key	No.	Size and description (use)
A	2	¾ x 1⅛ x 9¾″ mahogany (frame top and bottom)
B	2	¾ x 1⅛ x 13⅛″ mahogany (frame sides)
C	1	¼ x 6⅛ x 9⅞″ mahogany plywood (top scroll)
D	1	¼ x 4⅞ x 9⅞″ mahogany plywood (bottom scroll)
E	2	¼ x 2 x 5¾″ mahogany plywood (side scroll)
F	2	¼ x 2 x 5¾″ mahogany plywood (side scroll)
G	4	⅛ x ¾ x 2¼″ hardwood mahogany (splines)
H	1	⅛ x 8⅛ x 11½″ mirror
I	1	⅛ x 9¼ x 12⅝″ hardboard (back panel)
J	4	½″ No. 6 flathead screws
K	2	No. 16 screw eyes
Misc.: Carpenter's glue, picture-hanging wire, wood filler, 220-grit sandpaper, red mahogany stain, clear finish.		

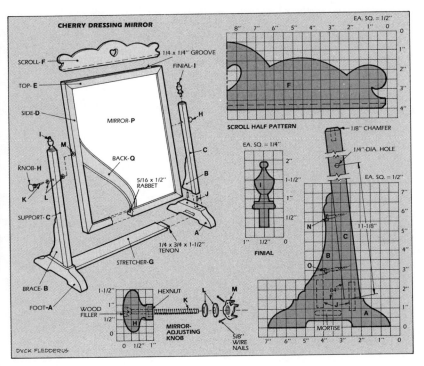

MATERIALS LIST
CHERRY DRESSING MIRROR

Key	No.	Size and description (use)
A	2	1⅜ x 2½ x 6½" cherry (base)
B	2	⅝ x 2⅝ x 5½" cherry (brace)
C	2	⅞ x 1⅛ x 14½" cherry (support)
D	2	⅞ x 1⅛ x 20" cherry (frame sides)
E	2	⅞ x 1⅛ x 16¾" cherry (frame top and bottom)
F	1	¼ x 3½ x 16¾" cherry (top scroll)
G	1	⅜ x 2 x 18¼" cherry (stretcher)
H	2	1 x 1½"-dia. cherry (knobs)
I	2	⅝"-dia. x 1⅞" cherry (finials)
J	4	⅜"-dia. x 1½" dowels
K	2	¼"-dia. x 2½" flathead stovebolts with nuts
L	4	¼"-dia. washers
M	2	¼"-dia. Teenuts
N	2	1" No. 8 roundhead screws
O	2	1½" No. 8 roundhead screws
P	1	⅛ x 15 x 18" mirror
Q	1	⅛ x 15 x 18" hardboard (back)

Misc.: Carpenter's glue, 1¾" 17-ga. wire brads, ⅝" 16-ga. wire nails, wood filler, polyurethane varnish, cherry stain.

series of ¼-in.-dia. holes and then chiseling out the waste.

Form the ⅛-in. chamfer on each support's top edge with a disc sander or block plane. Then, bore a ¼-in.-dia. hole in each support's top for installing the finials. Also, bore a ¼-in.-dia. hole through each support's side for installing the mirror adjusting knobs as shown.

Cut the bottoms of the supports and braces at a 6° angle (84° angle along the vertical plane). Then, attach the braces to the supports as shown. Use a doweling jig to bore each brace's bottom edge for two ⅜-in.-dia. wood dowels. The rear dowels are bored slightly deeper than the front dowels.

Transfer the braces' dowel hole locations to the two foot pieces using dowel centers. Bore ⅜-in.-dia. holes into the feet on these points. In this case, the rear dowels are bored into each foot *shallower* than the front dowels. This is to avoid boring into the foot pieces' mortises.

Glue and insert the dowels into the braces and then glue the braces onto the feet. The vertical support members are now completed, but they're not joined by the stretcher until after the mirror's frame is assembled and installed.

Before assembling the mirror's frame, bore a ⁵⁄₁₆-in.-dia. hole in each frame's side for installing Teenuts. See the instructions for the pine dressing mirror for installing the Teenuts and the mirror adjusting knobs.

Glue and nail the frame together with 1¾-in., 17-ga. wire nails at the corners. Clamp the frame square until the glue dries. Then, glue the decorative scroll into the frame's top groove. Assemble the support members to the frame by screwing the mirror adjusting knobs through the supports and into the frame's Teenuts. Tighten the mirror adjusting knobs to hold the supports parallel to the frame's sides. Cut the stretcher to equal the exact distance between the two feet. Dry-fit the stretcher to be sure its length and tenons fit properly. Make any necessary adjustments before gluing and final assembly.

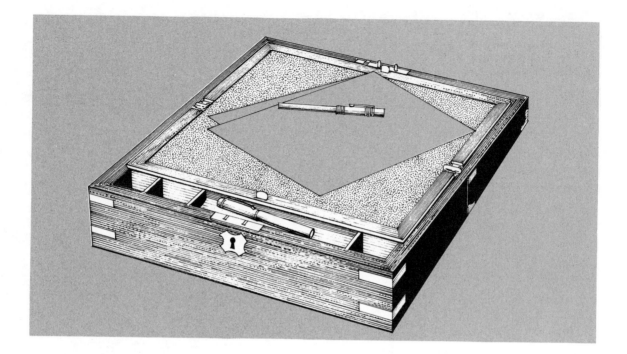

Classic lap desk

■ THIS MAHOGANY lap desk is a close reproduction of Mark Twain's desk, now in his collection at Elmira College in New York. This little piece of furniture must have played a significant role in Twain's daily life. Perhaps on the velvet panel he wrote *The Adventures of Tom Sawyer*. The compartments may have held the notes for *Life on the Mississippi*.

Today, a lap desk is still a convenient box to store the essentials for writing. When opened, the slanted, velvet-covered panels provide a handy writing surface.

Building the basic cabinet

The corners of the lap desk are mitered so they show no end grain. Glue and nail the front, back and ends; then add the top and bottom. Be careful to locate corner nails where they won't interfere with sawing the box into two parts. On the hinged side keep nails far enough from the sawed edges so they won't touch the hinge screws.

WITH FEW VARIATIONS, this lap desk is reproduced from the one mark twain used. The original desk is among the best in quality of workmanship seen in antique shops and museums today. Changes from the original piece incorporated into the copy include the brass corners of the lid (ones similar to the original weren't available), the size of the box and the material in the top. The copy is ¾ in. deeper from front to back to store 8½ in.-wide paper. Mahogany plywood is used in the top. If 10-in.-wide solid mahogany, as in the original, is readily available, you can plane it to ¼-in. thickness. Compartments provide storage for supplies.

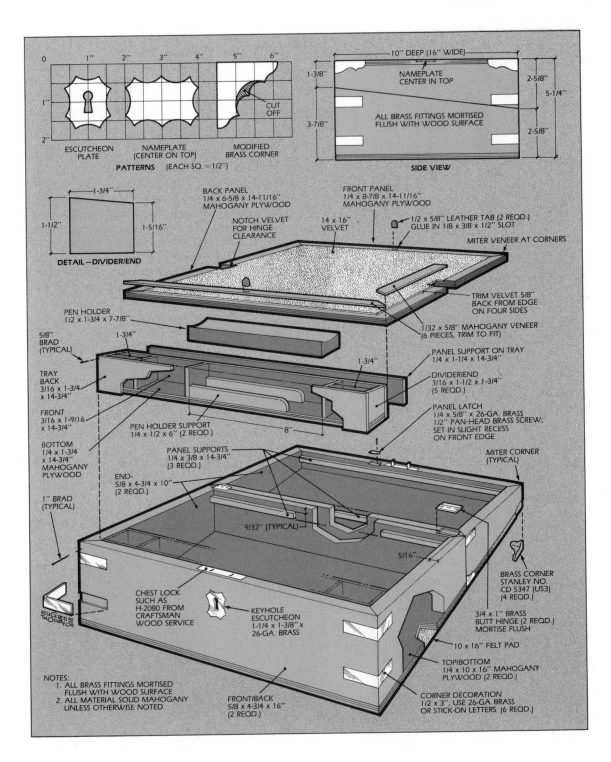

ESCUTCHEON PLATE

NAMEPLATE (CENTER ON TOP)

MODIFIED BRASS CORNER

PATTERNS (EACH SQ. = 1/2")

10" DEEP (16" WIDE)

NAMEPLATE CENTER IN TOP

1-3/8"

2-5/8"

5-1/4"

3-7/8"

ALL BRASS FITTINGS MORTISED FLUSH WITH WOOD SURFACE

2-5/8"

SIDE VIEW

1-3/4"

1-1/2"

1-5/16"

DETAIL—DIVIDER/END

BACK PANEL
1/4 x 6-5/8 x 14-11/16"
MAHOGANY PLYWOOD

FRONT PANEL
1/4 x 8-7/8 x 14-11/16"
MAHOGANY PLYWOOD

NOTCH VELVET FOR HINGE CLEARANCE

14 x 16"
VELVET

1/2 x 5/8" LEATHER TAB (2 REQD.)
GLUE IN 1/8 x 3/8 x 1/2" SLOT

MITER VENEER AT CORNERS

TRIM VELVET 5/8" BACK FROM EDGE ON FOUR SIDES

PEN HOLDER
1/2 x 1-3/4 x 7-7/8"

1-3/4"

1/32 x 5/8" MAHOGANY VENEER
(6 PIECES, TRIM TO FIT)

5/8" BRAD (TYPICAL)

1-3/4"

1-3/4"

PANEL SUPPORT ON TRAY
1/4 x 1-1/4 x 14-3/4"

TRAY BACK
3/16 x 1-3/4 x 14-3/4"

DIVIDER/END
3/16 x 1-1/2 x 1-3/4"
(5 REQD.)

FRONT
3/16 x 1-9/16 x 14-3/4"

PEN HOLDER SUPPORT
1/4 x 1/2 x 6" (2 REQD.)

8"

PANEL LATCH
1/4 x 5/8" x 26-GA. BRASS
1/2" PAN-HEAD BRASS SCREW;
SET IN SLIGHT RECESS
ON FRONT EDGE

BOTTOM
1/4 x 1-3/4 x 14-3/4"
MAHOGANY PLYWOOD

PANEL SUPPORTS
1/4 x 3/8 x 14-3/4"
(3 REQD.)

END—
5/8 x 4-3/4 x 10"
(2 REQD.)

MITER CORNER (TYPICAL)

1" BRAD (TYPICAL)

9/32" (TYPICAL)

5/16"

BRASS CORNER
STANLEY NO.
CD 5347 (US3)
(4 REQD.)

CHEST LOCK SUCH AS
H-2080 FROM CRAFTSMAN
WOOD SERVICE

KEYHOLE ESCUTCHEON
1-1/4 x 1-3/8" x 26-GA. BRASS

3/4 x 1" BRASS
BUTT HINGE (2 REQD.)
MORTISE FLUSH

10 x 16" FELT PAD

TOP/BOTTOM
1/4 x 10 x 16" MAHOGANY
PLYWOOD (2 REQD.)

NOTES:
1. ALL BRASS FITTINGS MORTISED FLUSH WITH WOOD SURFACE
2. ALL MATERIAL SOLID MAHOGANY UNLESS OTHERWISE NOTED

FRONT/BACK
5/8 x 4-3/4 x 16"
(2 REQD.)

CORNER DECORATION
1/2 x 3"; USE 26-GA. BRASS
OR STICK-ON LETTERS (6 REQD.)

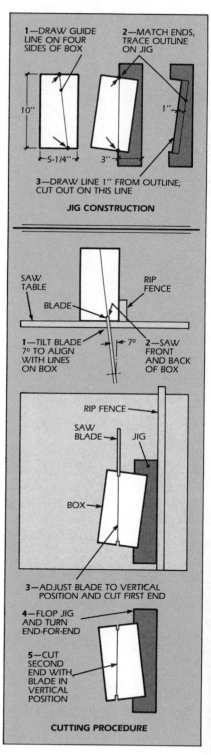

1—DRAW GUIDE LINE ON FOUR SIDES OF BOX

2—MATCH ENDS, TRACE OUTLINE ON JIG

10"

5-1/4"

3"

1"

3—DRAW LINE 1" FROM OUTLINE; CUT OUT ON THIS LINE

JIG CONSTRUCTION

SAW TABLE

RIP FENCE

BLADE

1—TILT BLADE 7° TO ALIGN WITH LINES ON BOX

7°

2—SAW FRONT AND BACK OF BOX

RIP FENCE

SAW BLADE

JIG

BOX

3—ADJUST BLADE TO VERTICAL POSITION AND CUT FIRST END

4—FLOP JIG AND TURN END-FOR-END

5—CUT SECOND END WITH BLADE IN VERTICAL POSITION

CUTTING PROCEDURE

After the glue dries, sand with 150- and 220-grit abrasive in a portable or stationary belt sander, or with an orbital sander. Using fine 220-grit sandpaper on a block, ease all corners. Then sand the top edges a little more. It's important to shape the wood to the slightly rounded brass corners.

Mark lines on the front, back and ends for separating the box into two parts (see drawings). You'll need to remove the guard from the table saw for this job. Tilt the blade about 7° from vertical, lower the blade so only ¾ in. extends above the table, and make the front and back cuts, using the rip fence. Make a simple jig to hold the box at the proper angle to the rip fence while making the diagonal end cuts. Move the blade back to the vertical position and use the jig against the rip fence to make these cuts. A fine-tooth plywood blade works well for this job.

Install the lock before gluing and nailing the tray in place. Chisel away the wood and shape the keyhole, following instructions supplied by the maker. A high-speed hand grinder with a flat end burr is helpful in doing the final smoothing.

Building the accessory tray

Rip ³⁄₁₆-in.-thick strips of mahogany on the table or radial-arm saw for the accessory tray.

WEAR SAFETY GOGGLES

TO PREVENT glued surfaces from sliding out of position, you should prebore holes before nailing. Take care not to use any nails near the diagonal cutline which divides the box into top and bottom.

MAKE THE LENGTHWISE CUTS AT a 7° angle (see drawings). Then return the blade to the vertical position and use a jig to make the two end cuts.

FIT THE LOCK into the front of the box. Remove most of the wood with a chisel then use a high-speed hand grinder in the finishing stages. You may prefer to do this job before you start assembling the desk.

USING A MALLET, ⅛- and ¼-in. wood chisels, remove the wood to a ¹⁄₃₂-in. depth. Fit the brass frequently to check depth.

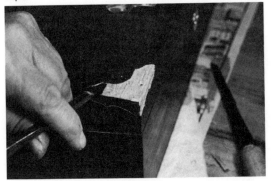

Sand both sides. Cut pieces to the dimensions shown and assemble, checking the fit inside the box. Make a concave insert to hold pens and pencils. Apply glue to the ends and to the side that's adjacent to the box and nail in place with a wire brad at each end.

Attach the other three panel support strips ⁹⁄₃₂ in. from the edge. Cut two ¼-in. mahogany panels to fit. Stain and apply satin finish polyurethane to the backs of both panels and to the entire assembly.

You can duplicate the original's slightly brownish mahogany stain by mixing ⅔ red mahogany to ⅓ special walnut. After the stain dries, fill nail holes with matching color.

Since mahogany is open-grained wood, you'll get a smoother surface if you next apply paste wood filler that has been tinted with the same stain used for the first coat. Follow instructions on the can, rubbing across the grain.

Follow up by using two or three coats of satin finish polyurethane. Do not apply stain or finish to the hinged edges because velvet will be glued to them later.

Installing the hinges

Using a sharp wood chisel to mark the locations and to pare away the wood, set the ¾ x 1-in. brass hinges in ⁵⁄₁₆ in. from the ends and flush with the surface. This allows for two thicknesses of velvet when the lap desk is closed. Bore the holes and then screw the hinges in place.

Installing the velvet

On the upper or unfinished side of the two panels, draw lines ⅝ in. from the edge, parallel to the ends and outsides of the opened box. With the panels in place, apply to the larger one a thin, smooth coating of glue, extending it just to the outside of the line you have drawn.

Lay the velvet in place, brushing out wrinkles. Coat the smaller panel with glue in the same way, draw the velvet fairly tight across the center, lay it on the glued surface of the smaller panel and brush out any wrinkles.

After the glue has dried, remove the panels from the box and use a steel straightedge and razor blade or sharp utility knife to remove excess cloth.

Cut mahogany veneer to shape with sharp household shears and glue it to the ⅝-in. margin around three sides of each panel. If you use carpenter's glue you'll have to clamp wood over each strip until it dries. Follow the maker's directions for contact cement. Stain and varnish the veneer trim and edges. Cut the slot and install leather tabs.

Trim the velvet to fit between the two hinges, apply glue to the box edges between the hinges and set the two panels in place. Press the velvet down on the glued edges and leave the box open until the glue is dry. Install the catch to hold the large panel when the box is opened. Glue a piece of felt or corduroy to the bottom of the lap desk so it won't scratch the surface you set it on.

Installing the brass trim

If you attach an escutcheon around the keyhole and stop right there, you will have a nice-looking lap desk. If you want an even more beautiful one, however—a reasonably true reproduction of the Mark Twain lap desk—you'll need to add some brass trimming: a name or initial plate, decorative escutcheon, brass corners and brass corner straps.

The corners and corner straps cannot be surface-mounted, as this would interfere with opening the lap desk to its fullest extent. A raised nameplate could scratch a tabletop. All brass should be flush-mounted.

Before you begin chiseling for the brass mountings, it's a good idea to practice on scrap wood. Use sharp ⅛-in. and ¼-in. wood chisels. Keep a cloth under the box to protect the finish and anchor the box with some blocking. As you work, keep both hands behind the sharp chisel edge.

Lay the brass corner (or other brass trim) in the proper location and outline it with an awl. Using the ⅛-in. wood chisel, bevel toward the part to be removed; cut straight down around the outline to establish the edge. Then remove enough wood within the boundary to permit the brass to fit evenly, flush with the wood surface.

On the corners, you'll find it necessary to make a new perimeter line just outside the original as you remove a layer of wood. After you fit each piece, remove it and apply a thin line of stain around the edge of the cut.

Secure all brass parts with contact cement. Apply it to the wood and to the back of the brass, wait for the period of time recommended by the maker and press the brass in place.

To make the ½ x 3-in. straps around each corner, you can use the same 26-ga. brass or you can purchase 3-in.-high brass stick-on sign letters. The letters save time and are difficult to differentiate from thicker brass. Cut portions of the letters to give you the dimensions you need and stick them in place. With the last piece of brass trim in place, you are ready to use the handsome lap desk.

SHOWN ABOVE is our reproduction of the mahogany clock that was in the Butler family home, where Lincoln stayed while starting his Springfield law practice. The original clock is now in the Lincoln home.

Lincoln legacy: two mantel clocks you can build

■ WE'VE GONE BACK into history to bring you two clocks that Abraham Lincoln must have checked time by during his early days as an aspiring young lawyer, and later as a U.S. statesman. The mahogany clock was in the Butler home where Lincoln stayed when opening his law practice in Springfield. Today, it is in the sitting room of the Lincoln Home National Historic Site in Springfield, Ill.

The back of the illustration in the pine clock bears an inscription by Lincoln's son Tad. To help you make your reproduction a faithful one, we've reproduced both this inscription and the decorative drawing.

There are minor differences between the original clocks (in the smaller photos) and the reproductions: The originals have 30-hour movements, while ours are eight-day clocks. The original movements are screwed to the backs of the cases. In the reproductions, we've mounted the movements on a sheet-metal faceplate. The winding arbors on the reproductions are at 6 o'clock, whereas on the originals they are at 3:00 and 11:00.

For both clocks, we selected an eight-day, spring-wound, pendulum movement. Modern hands come with the mechanism, but for more authenticity you'll probably want the older styles we've specified. These hands, plus the appropriate paper dial faces, are also available. You merely glue the paper dial to the metal backing plate.

There are, however, many other types of clock movements that you might wish to consider, such as quartz, electric or battery models.

Building the pine clock

Tad's pine clock has a fairly straightforward rectangular cabinet. Rip the base stock in one piece and cut the bevel before dividing it into the three parts. Then cut the grooves in the two side-pieces. Next, rip the sides for the case and cut the rabbets, using a table saw, router or jointer.

Glue and nail the bottom and base pieces so the assembly is square. Clamp if needed. Sand the exposed edges of the remaining pieces with 100-grit paper. Glue and clamp the sides to the base, making sure the sides are square. Cut and attach the back, then the top.

Rip stock for the door and make the rabbet to hold the glass. Sand the inside edges with 100-grit paper. Glue up the door; when it's dry, cut the crosspieces and glue them in place. Sand the upper and lower door edges at a 2° or 3° inward angle (bevel) so the door will close smoothly.

Sand all parts, breaking the corners, dust and wipe with a tack cloth. We applied a dark walnut stain to the wood. When the stain is thoroughly dry, rub on several coats of French polish (20 percent boiled linseed oil and 80 percent orange shellac), using 4/0 steel wool. Next, buff with carnauba wax.

You can make pin hinges from 20-ga. brass to mount the door. Cut two hinges as shown in the drawing. Bore a hole for a small brass nail. File the hinges smooth and bend to shape. Use a No. 60 bit to bore hinge-mounting holes in the door. Bend the lower hinge upward slightly, so that the door doesn't rub on the base.

Carefully cut the paper face to fit the opening. Cut the sheet metal to fit the face. Bore holes for the hands, winding arbor and mounting screws in the metal. Apply the paper face to the metal with rubber cement.

Paint flowers at four corners of the dial with light green paint to create the decorative tole design shown on the original. File the paper away from the arbor holes with a round file. Mount the movement to the metal faceplate and screw the assembly into the case. Cut wood strips to hold glass. Attach glass with epoxy resin, glue train art and cement wood strips.

Finally, shape the door catch of 20-ga. brass and attach it with a ⅜-in. brass brad. Nail another brad to the door to receive the catch. Marks on the original indicate that the clock was hung on the wall at one time. If you wish, snip a brass hanger to shape, bore holes as needed and fasten with brads to the case back.

Building the Butler clock

Before you begin construction on the mahogany clock, study the drawing carefully. Start by ripping the stock for the sides and top. Round the front edges as shown in the drawing with a spokeshave or other shaping tool.

Cut the bottom to size. Then rip base stock and round its edge as shown before cutting individual lengths. Cut the rabbets and the miters for the front corners. Assemble the sides to the base with glue; when dry, glue and nail the base to the bottom. Bore pilot holes before driving any nails to prevent splitting the hardwood. Miter the three top pieces, and glue and nail them in place. To complete the case, cut the backpiece, and glue and nail it in place.

To construct the door, rip stock and cut the pieces to size, carefully trimming the ends to the correct angles. Then cut grooves for the splines. Notch the door catch on the left sidepiece, and cut panel J (see art) to size.

Dry-assemble and test-fit the door before you glue all of the parts. After gluing, sand with 120-grit paper, beveling the edges to a slight inward angle so the door will close easily.

Next, glue a filler strip (L) on the inside of the front at the bottom, and glue in the mounting blocks (E). You can make the small quarter-round molding in front of the mirror by ripping a ½-in. dowel in half, then the halves into quarters. Paint the quarter-round with gilding.

We finished the case by dipping it and the door (not yet attached) in a solution of 1 tablespoon of lye to 1 gal. of water. *Note:* Use extreme caution when working with lye. Wear goggles, gloves and long sleeves.

The lye acts as a bleach, lightening the tone of the wood and helping to get rid of the purplish tinge that mahogany often has. When the wood reaches the desired shade, wash the case off with water and wipe it dry. When completely dry, apply French polish, a mixture of 20-percent boiled linseed oil and 80-percent orange shellac, rubbed in with 4/0 steel wool.

Fill in the nail holes with the appropriate shade of wax stick and buff with carnauba wax.

Cut a latch from 20-ga. brass and attach it to the knob with epoxy cement. Cut a slot in the case for the catch. Mark and cut the paper dial

PRIMITIVE but handsome pine mantel clock features the train drawing below. The drawing is actual size (see original clock in the photo on the left), so you can clip it from this page.

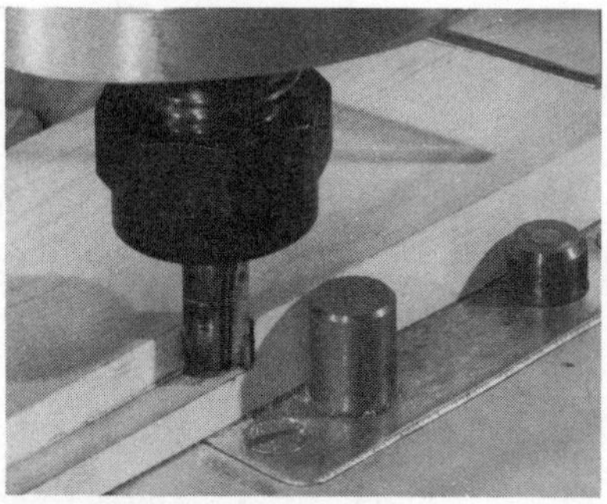

EDGE RABBETS for sides, bottom and door frame can be cut with table saw, router or router in overhead arm.

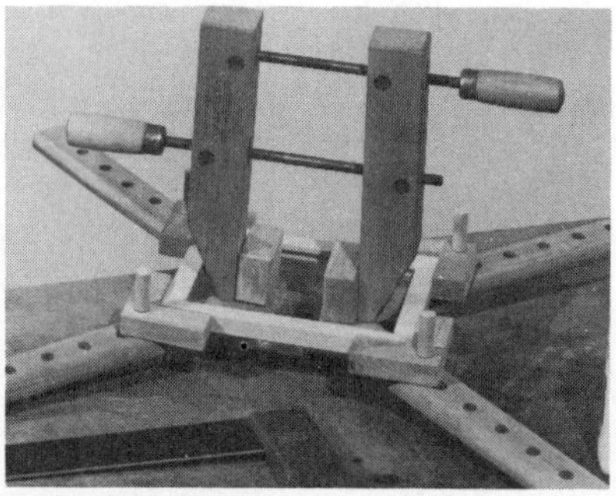

GLUE AND CLAMP mitered door-frame pieces. When dry, bore pilot holes in corners to reinforce with 3d nails.

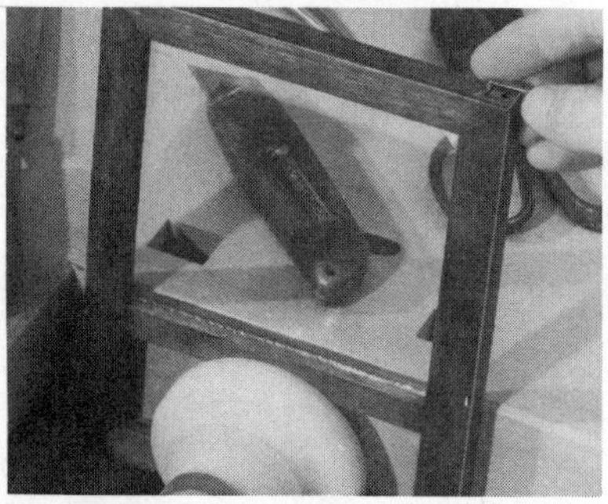

PIN HINGES for door are reproduced from thin, polished brass. See text and drawing for installation.

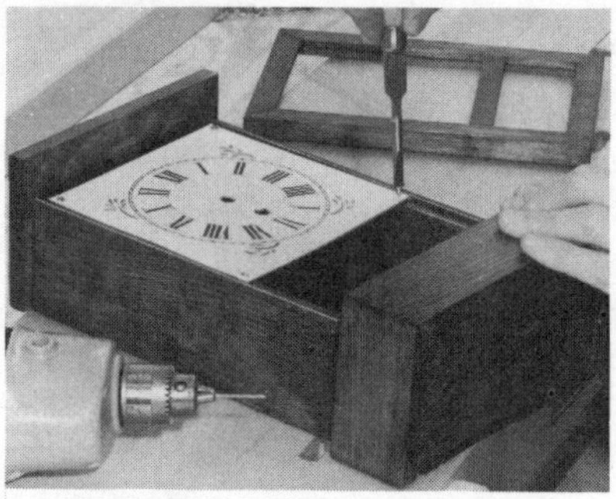

PAPER CLOCK FACE is glued to metal backing plate, and plate is fastened into rabbets in case with small screws.

MATERIALS LIST—TAD'S PINE CLOCK

Key	Amt.	Size and description (use)
A	1	½ x 3½ x 6⅝" pine (top)
B	2	½ x 2⅝ x 10⅛" pine (side)
C	2	½ x 2 x 3½" pine (base side)
D	1	½ x 2 x 7" pine (base front)
E	1	⅜ x 2¾ x 6½" pine (bottom)
F	1	¼ x 5½ x 10½" pine (back)
G	2	9/16 x 11/16 x 6" pine (door top/bottom)
H	2	9/16 x 11/16 x 10⅛" pine (door side)
I	1	7/16 x ½ x 5" pine (crosspiece)
J	1	⅛ x ⅝ x 4⅝" pine (crosspiece)
K	2	⅛ x ¼ x 4 15/16" (glass retainer)
L	1	⅛ x ¼ x 4 15/16" (glass retainer)
M	1	4 5/16 x 4 5/16" single-strength glass (for clock)
N	1	1 5/16 x 4 5/16" single-strength glass (for picture)
O	2	¼ x 1" 20-gauge brass (hinge)
P	1	1 x 2" 20-gauge brass (door catch)
Q	1	⅝ x ¾" 20-gauge brass (hanger)
R	1	2 x 5" (picture, clip from magazine)
S	1	4¼-dia. dial with ⅝" Roman numerals (paper clock dial)
T	1	5 11/16 x 5 11/16" 20-gauge steel metal (metal backing for clock dial)
U	1	Urgo 8-day pendulum clock movement
V	2	1⅜" and 2⅛" serpentine clock hands

Misc.: ½" No. 4 fh brass screws (4); ½" brass brads; epoxy cement; 3d finishing nails; stain; French polish (80% orange shellac and 20% boiled linseed oil).

face to fit the opening, then use it as a pattern for cutting the sheet-metal backing. Bore holes in the metal for the hands, winding arbor and mounting screws. Apply the paper dial to the metal with rubber cement, and trim the paper away from the holes with a round file. Then fasten the clock movement to the metal faceplate with the grommets provided and screw the plate into the case.

INSCRIPTION by Lincoln's son Tad can be clipped out and pasted behind the door.

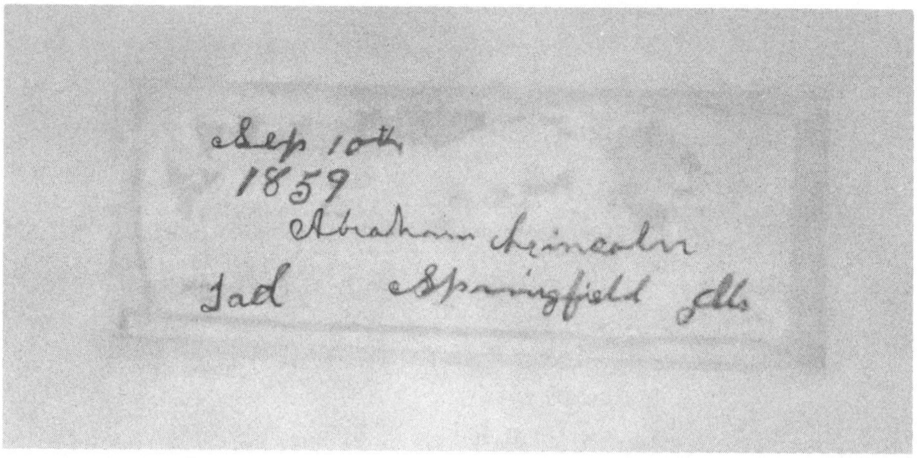

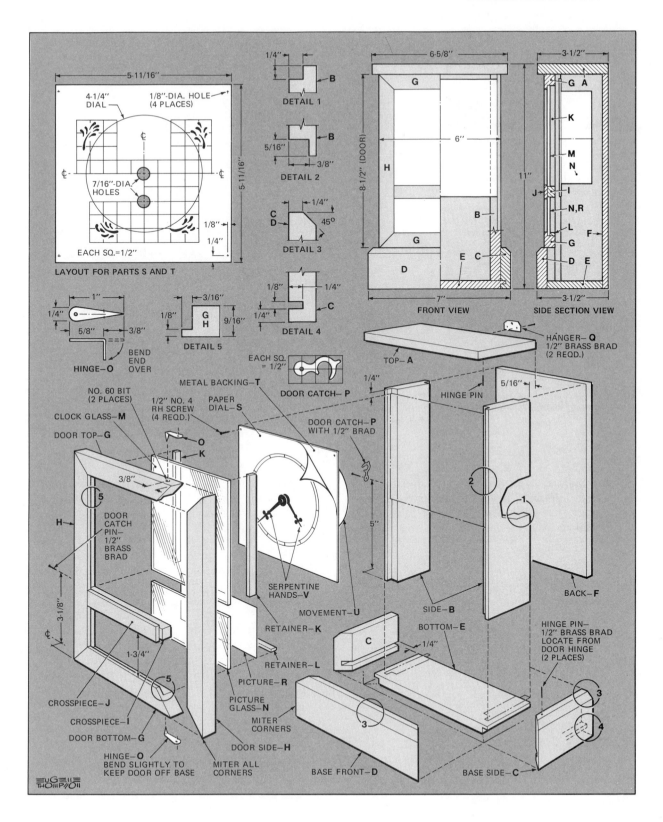

5-11/16"

4-1/4"
DIAL

1/8"-DIA. HOLE
(4 PLACES)

7/16"-DIA.
HOLES

5-11/16"

1/8"

1/4"

EACH SQ.=1/2"

LAYOUT FOR PARTS S AND T

1/4"

B

DETAIL 1

5/16"

3/8"

B

DETAIL 2

C
D

1/4"

45°

DETAIL 3

1/8"

1/4"

1/4"

C

DETAIL 4

1"

1/4"

5/8"

3/8"

HINGE—O

BEND
END
OVER

3/16"

1/8"

G
H

9/16"

DETAIL 5

EACH SQ.
= 1/2"

DOOR CATCH— P

6-5/8"

G

6"

H

G

B

G

E C

D

7"

FRONT VIEW

8-1/2" (DOOR)

3-1/2"

G A

K

M

N

J

I

N,R

L

F

G

D E

11"

3-1/2"

SIDE SECTION VIEW

TOP— A

HANGER— Q
1/2" BRASS BRAD
(2 REQD.)

1/4"

HINGE PIN

5/16"

NO. 60 BIT
(2 PLACES)

METAL BACKING— T

CLOCK GLASS— M

1/2" NO. 4
RH SCREW
(4 REQD.)

PAPER
DIAL— S

DOOR TOP— G

3/8"

DOOR CATCH— P
WITH 1/2" BRAD

O

K

2

1

5

H

DOOR
CATCH
PIN—
1/2"
BRASS
BRAD

5"

3-1/8"

1-3/4"

5

CROSSPIECE— J

CROSSPIECE— I

DOOR BOTTOM— G

HINGE—O
BEND SLIGHTLY TO
KEEP DOOR OFF BASE

SERPENTINE
HANDS— V

MOVEMENT— U

RETAINER— K

RETAINER— L

PICTURE— R

PICTURE
GLASS— N

MITER
CORNERS

MITER ALL
CORNERS

C

BASE FRONT— D

BOTTOM— E

1/4"

3

SIDE— B

BACK— F

HINGE PIN—
1/2" BRASS BRAD
LOCATE FROM
DOOR HINGE
(2 PLACES)

3

4

BASE SIDE— C

EUGENE
THOMPSON

CUT GROOVES for splines in door-frame pieces. To prevent narrow wood from slipping through blade slot, run scrap of ⅛-in. hardboard partway through saw to make a temporary surface.

AFTER CUTTING and grooving door-frame pieces, rout out recess for catch.

TO FINISH the mahogany clock, wood was immersed in a lye solution. When dry, it was polished, using 4/0 steel wool and a mixture of one part boiled linseed oil with four parts orange shellac.

FIRST, CUT paper clock face to fit the case, then use paper cutout to transfer shape onto sheet metal. Cut and bore metal and glue paper to it. Movement mounts on back with brass nuts.

MATERIALS LIST—BUTLER CLOCK

Key	Amt.	Size and description (use)
A	2	⅝ x 1⅝ x 3⅜" mahogany (base side)
B	1	⅝ x 1⅝ x 7" mahogany (base front)
C	2	½ x 3 x 7¼" mahogany (side)
D	3	½ x 3 x 2½" mahogany (top)
E	2	½ x ¾ x 4" (mounting block)
F	1	⅜ x 2¾ x 6¼" (bottom)
G	2	⅜ x ¹¹⁄₁₆ x 5¾" mahogany (door side)
H	1	⅜ x ¹¹⁄₁₆ x 5" mahogany (door bottom)
I	3	⅜ x ¹¹⁄₁₆ x 2¹⁄₁₆" mahogany (door top)
J	1	⅜ x 2 x 3⅝" mahogany (door panel)
K	1	¼ x 5½ x 9⅛" (back)
L	1	¼ x 1¼ x 5" (filler)
M	2	⅛ x ¾ x ¾" (spline)
N	3	⅛ x ⁵⁄₁₆ x 3" (spline, trim to fit)
O	2	3⅝" quarter-round molding for top/bottom (cut quarter rounds from ½"-dia. dowel x 6")
P	2	1¼" quarter-round molding for sides (cut from dowel as above)
Q	2	¾ x ¾ x 1½" (glue block)
R	1	⅛ x 1¼ x 3⅝" mirror
S	1	3⁷⁄₁₆"-dia. single-strength glass (for clock)
T	1	4"-dia. brass clock bezel
U	3	¼ x ⅝" 20-gauge brass (retainer)
V	2	½ x ¾" brass butt hinge
W	1	½ x ½" brass knob
X	1	⁵⁄₁₆ x ⅝" 20-gauge brass (door latch)
Y	1	Urgo 8-day pendulum clock movement
Z	1	3½"-dia. paper dial face
AA	1	5 x 5" 20-gauge sheet metal (metal backing for clock dial)
BB	1	1¾" and 1½" spade clock hands

Misc.: ¼" No. 4 rh screws (4); 3d finish nails; ⅜" brads; extra grommet for winding-arbor hole; gold gilding.

Mortise hinges into the door and fasten the door in place. Cement the quarter-round molding to the mirror and the mirror into the door with epoxy.

Also apply small dabs of epoxy to hold the glass in the brass bezel. Install the bezel in the door, attach the hands and pendulum, and your clock is finished.

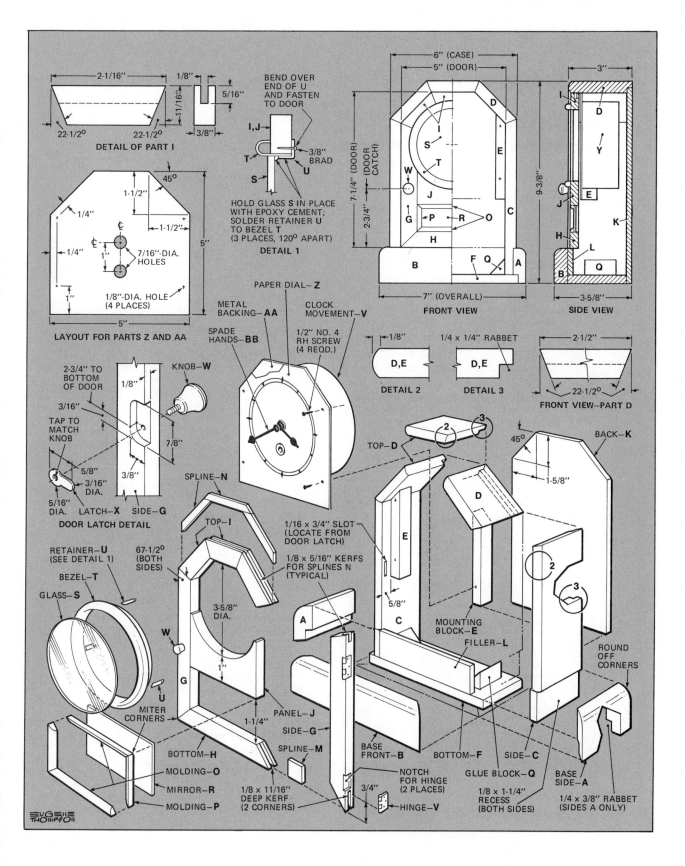

Appliance repair

■ THIS SECTION CONTAINS HELP about most aspects of repair and regular upkeep of the major appliances in your home. Here's a list of what you'll find:

Appliance basic checklist is a quick trouble-shooting guide to the most fundamental information everyone should have about their appliances. Included also are some suggestions for help if you get in over your head.

How to fix a food freezer will help you demystify that big white box and its condenser, compressor, and thermostats. Charts and diagrams help you understand the basics of a typical freezer components and operations. You'll also

find help on what you can do to keep it running smoothly.

How to fix an electric dryer gives you charts and diagrams to help you make your way successfully through the dark insides of your electric dryer. All electric dryers operate with the same basic components for the common functions described.

How to fix a gas dryer goes beyond the basic dryer situations to the specific solutions to gas problems that you can fix. Illustrations of the dryer and troubleshooting charts help you escape from that pile of dirty laundry.

How to fix an automatic washer explains common washer components so you'll know what's happening. Guides to specific malfunctions of this complicated machine will help you keep it running, or fix any problem with ordinary household tools.

How to fix your dishwasher clearly illustrates the causes of dishwasher afflictions and suggests actions you can take to make your kitchen chores a little easier again. You'll see all the controls and components in clear detail with charts to pinpoint your specific problems.

MODERN HOUSEHOLD appliances are crucial to the quality of life we have grown to enjoy. With less effort as time goes on, we can prepare meals, wash clothes or conveniently store quantities of fresh food—all with the aid of these magnificent machines. And new technology develops even more sophisticated appliances every day, such as these electronically controlled units. While computer brains and diagnostic cycles will help us operate and maintain these new models, they have the same requirements for care as machines produced for the last several decades.

How to troubleshoot a water heater will help you avoid difficulties with one of the home's most forgotten but important appliances. With a little knowledge and these suggestions, you'll stay in hot water.

How to troubleshoot your electric range is a complete guide to potential problems and ways to eliminate them. Lists of causes are matched with possible solutions, and detailed diagrams illustrate the components. Careful study may prevent future panic.

How to repair a garbage disposer is the first place to look should you ever be unable to operate this important piece of kitchen machinery. It tells you exactly how different types work, and just how to proceed with your repairs and service.

Refrigerator tune-up cuts operating costs is a great home maintenance project that you can do with tools from your kitchen drawers and save real energy dollars. You can ensure longer life for your refrigerator by following these basic procedures.

In addition, **small appliance repair** is treated in a section of Volume 22. There you'll find help on fixing household appliances from food processors to vacuum cleaners.

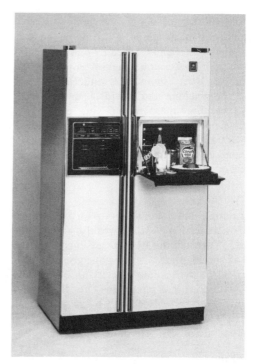

Appliance basic checklist

■ APPLIANCES PERFORM better and last longer when they are kept clean, dry, level, properly wired and treated with a little preventive maintenance.

Machines with dirty filters or broken gaskets have to work harder to do their task, leading to overheating or overloading components. Moisture brings rust and corrosion to parts, structure and connections, causing early problems. Machines that are not level place undue strain on motors, bearings and pumps inside. Poor wiring and corroded connections can cause control mechanisms to malfunction frequently, and may pose a fire threat. Most appliances will operate efficiently and last longer if you occasionally take 60 seconds to follow the maintenance suggestions in the manual that came with your appliance. Here's a list of basic preventive maintenance chores you can begin with.

Refrigerators

Drain holes in refrigerators can be unclogged with a pipe cleaner and cleaned by pouring a cup of warm soapy water down them from inside the refrigerator. Dust accumulates underneath and behind the machine and retards operating efficiency; vacuum there when you clean the kitchen. Leaky door gaskets add dollars to each utility bill. If there are gaps and cracks, purchase a new gasket. Just pull the old one off and push the new one into its channel.

Electric ranges

Any burner that doesn't heat up on an electric range, or those that heat up weakly, should be replaced. Turn off the burner, let it cool, then pull it off the coupling. The new one you can buy at the dealer's pushes into place. Unless you are handy with electrical repair, switches that malfunction should be replaced only by an appliance repair professional. The 220 volts most electric ranges operate on can give quite a jolt.

Gas ranges

Because of the danger of leaking gas, major problems with a gas range should be tackled only by professionals. You can, however, clean or adjust the pilot light.

Washers

Washers are complicated devices with many mechanical and electrical systems. Treat them with care and respect. Follow the manufacturer's instructions for use and maintenance. Most important is cleaning the filters and balancing your loads to avoid overloading pumps and bearings. Check to see that all four feet of the washer are firmly supported and that the machine is level. Spin cycles turn fast and can damage an out-of-level or poorly supported machine.

Dryers

Make sure your dryer is level, and check and clean lint filters frequently. Dryers are simple machines and belts wear out only after years of service. Most manufacturers provide detailed instructions, so you can install a new one yourself.

Dishwashers

Load dishwashers carefully so that dishes are separated from each other and with room for cleaning water to pass. The most common problem is oversudsing. You can prevent this by using the correct amount and type of detergent specified by the manufacturer. Never use laundry soap.

Help by phone

Most major manufacturers now have toll-free phone numbers for do-it-yourself assistance. Your machine will appear on their computer screen when you tell them the model number. They can troubleshoot for you and suggest repairs any handy person can do. And they can send a replacement manual if yours is lost. At least one major manufacturer publishes quick-fix repair manuals for washers, dryers, refrigerators, dishwashers and kitchen ranges.

The bottom line

If any machine is old and troublesome, think about replacing it. All new appliances are designed to use energy more efficiently, so they will cost less to operate. If a repair will not give you at least a year of extended life and will be more than one-quarter the cost of a new machine, then replace it. With new features and lower operating costs, a new appliance may be a better investment. On the other hand, by following a regular program of care and maintenance yourself, you may be able to extend the life of your appliances, making frequent replacement less necessary.

Food freezer repair

■ MANY OF THE PROBLEMS that may arise with home food freezers can be dealt with by consulting the 12 troubleshooting charts on this page and the following pages. Many falsely believe that the home handyman cannot begin to understand his food freezer. Troubles that involve the sealed refrigeration system should be left to a qualified serviceman, but it will be helpful if the homeowner can recognize the symptoms when they occur.

In a normal system, refrigerant in a gaseous state is pumped by the compressor into the condenser, where it cools and changes into a liquid. It then passes through the extremely narrow capillary tube that leads to the evaporator. The change to larger tubing diameter at the evaporator inlet reduces the pressure on the refrigerant, allowing it to boil at low temperature, absorbing heat from the area surrounding the evaporator as it does. The vapor that results is drawn into the compressor to begin a new cycle.

During normal operation, the condenser will feel warm, the evaporator cold and the suction line from evaporator to compressor will be cool or at about room temperature. To work properly, the system must contain a specific amount (charge) of refrigerant and its lines must be unobstructed.

When a system is undercharged, the freezer lacks normal frost accumulation on walls or evaporator coil. The compressor runs continually or for longer periods than normal, drawing less current than normal, and temperatures inside the freezer rise. Evaporator and condenser both feel warmer than in normal operation.

Leaks cause undercharge

Undercharge is most commonly the result of a leak. Oil stains around a joint will indicate a leak. Test for leaks by brushing a soapy water solution over joints on the system's high side (compressor, condenser, capillary) while the freezer is running, over joints on the low side (evaporator, suction line) while it is off. Any sign of bubbling at a joint indicates a leak.

When a system is overcharged, frost accumu-

Compressor does not run

POSSIBLE CAUSES	WHAT TO TRY
1. Blown fuse or tripped circuit breaker.	Replace fuse or reset circuit breaker.
2. Defective relay.	Test for continuity between terminals L and R, S and L. Replace relay if there is no reading between L and R, or if there is a reading between S and L.
3. Defective overload protector.	Remove wires from overload protector and test for continuity across terminals. Replace overload protector if there is no reading at room temperature.
4. Defective temperature control (thermostat).	Remove wires from thermostat, turn control to coldest setting and test for continuity across terminals. Replace control if there is no reading.
5. Defective defrost timer.	Remove wires from defrost timer, and test for continuity across terminals for timer motor, defrost and compressor circuits (refer to unit's wiring diagram). Replace the timer if a circuit is open.
6. Defective compressor.	Direct-test compressor with test jumper. Have it replaced if it fails to operate properly.

Typical freezer components

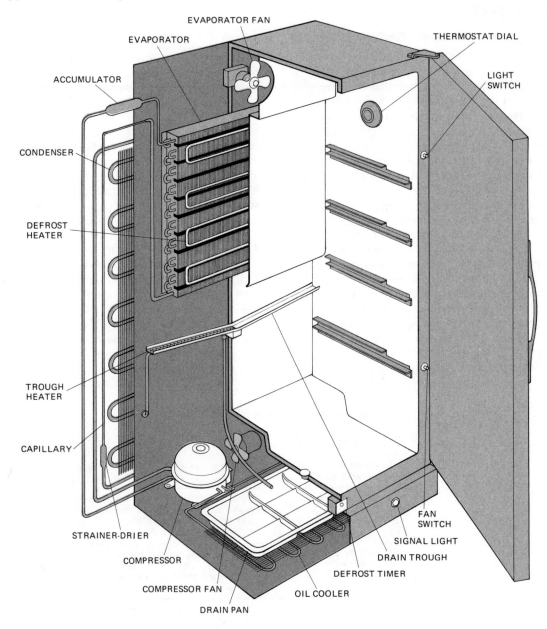

EVAPORATOR FAN

EVAPORATOR

ACCUMULATOR

CONDENSER

DEFROST HEATER

TROUGH HEATER

CAPILLARY

STRAINER-DRIER

COMPRESSOR

COMPRESSOR FAN

DRAIN PAN

OIL COOLER

DEFROST TIMER

DRAIN TROUGH

SIGNAL LIGHT

FAN SWITCH

THERMOSTAT DIAL

LIGHT SWITCH

lates on the suction line between evaporator and compressor, and the compressor may run longer than normal or continually. Overcharge will exist only when the sealed system has been broken into. In the case of either undercharge or overcharge, the system must be evacuated and recharged with the correct amount of refrigerant. This is a job for a qualified service professional who has the knowledge and the equipment to do a good job.

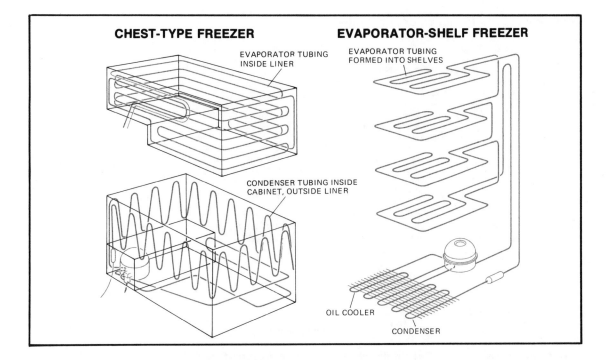

CHEST-TYPE FREEZER

EVAPORATOR TUBING
INSIDE LINER

CONDENSER TUBING INSIDE
CABINET, OUTSIDE LINER

EVAPORATOR-SHELF FREEZER

EVAPORATOR TUBING
FORMED INTO SHELVES

OIL COOLER

CONDENSER

Compressor cycles on overload protector

POSSIBLE CAUSES	WHAT TO TRY
1. Low voltage.	Test voltage at wall outlet with a voltmeter. This should be within 10 percent of normal. If it's low, call power company.
2. Poor air circulation over condenser.	If condenser is dirty, vacuum-clean the coil and surrounding area.
3. Defective relay.	See No. 2 in chart titled "Compressor does not run."
4. Restricted system.	If signs of restriction (see text) are present, contact a qualified service professional.

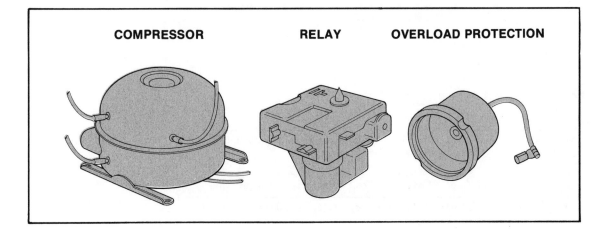

COMPRESSOR   **RELAY**   **OVERLOAD PROTECTION**

Compressor runs too much or constantly

POSSIBLE CAUSES	WHAT TO TRY
1. Thermostat is set too high or feeler bulb has worked loose.	Adjust thermostat to a warmer setting. Make sure that feeler bulb is secure in mounting.
2. Poor air circulation at condenser.	If condenser is dirty, use a vacuum cleaner on the coil and surrounding area.
3. Poor door seal.	Close the door on a dollar bill; there should be a slight tug when the bill is pulled out. If not, check the door and hinges for warp—if present, loosen the door-liner screws, push the door in until it seats against the gasket and retighten liner screws.
4. Undercharged or restricted system.	If signs of undercharge or restriction are present (see text) call a qualified service professional.

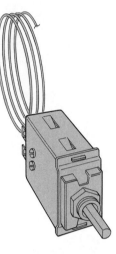

THERMOSTAT

CAUTION: Be sure power is turned *off* before you handle components. Make all continuity tests with power *off*. When using a test lamp, keep power *off* while connecting and disconnecting the lamp. Use your manufacturer's manual to locate components, and use only replacement parts that meet his specifications. Do not open the refrigerant system.

Freezer compartment too warm

POSSIBLE CAUSES	WHAT TO TRY
1. Poor door seal.	See No. 3 in chart titled "Compressor runs too much or constantly" above.
2. Defective freezer fan.	Disconnect wires from the fan and direct-test fan motor. Replace the motor if it fails to operate properly.
3. Defective defrost heater.	Disconnect wires from the heater and test it for continuity. Replace heater if no reading can be obtained.
4. Door opened too often.	Limit the number of door openings to reduce the amount of air at room temperature that can enter the freezer.
5. Defective defrost timer.	See chart titled "Compressor does not run."
6. Freezer overloaded with unfrozen food.	Add no more than 10 percent of freezer capacity at one time; remove some food or add dry ice.
7. Interior light on.	Push light-switch button in; the light should go out. If it does not, remove switch and test it for continuity. There should be a reading with button out, none with button in. Replace switch if defective.

Freezer does not defrost

POSSIBLE CAUSES	WHAT TO TRY
1. Insufficient time allowed for defrosting (manual).	Normal time to soften frost is 10 to 15 minutes. Repeat defrost cycle.
2. Defective defrost timer.	See chart titled "Compressor does not run."
3. Defective defrost heater	See chart titled "Compressor does not run."

Freezer fan does not run

POSSIBLE CAUSES	WHAT TO TRY
1. Freezer defrosting.	Normal. Check again later.
2. Defective fan switch.	Remove wires from switch, test for continuity. There should be a reading with button in, none with button out. Replace switch if defective.
3. Defective fan motor.	Disconnect wires and direct-test fan motor. Replace it if it fails to operate properly.
4. Defective defrost timer.	See chart, "Compressor does not run."
5. Loose or defective wiring.	Check wiring against manufacturer's diagram. Tighten any loose wires.

DEFROST TIMERS

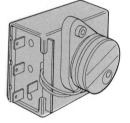

Water freezes in drain trough

POSSIBLE CAUSES	WHAT TO TRY
1. Defective drain-trough heater.	Remove wires and test heater for continuity.
2. Defective defrost timer.	See chart "Compressor does not run."
3. Loose or defective wiring.	Check wiring against manufacturer's diagram. Tighten any loose wires.

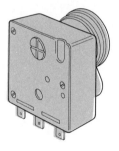

Moisture condenses on cabinet or door

POSSIBLE CAUSES	WHAT TO TRY
1. Poor door seal.	See chart titled "Compressor runs too much or constantly."
2. Defective door heater.	Disconnect wires from door heater and test for continuity. Replace it if there is no reading.
3. Door opened too often.	Limit number of door openings to keep air at room temperature out of freezer.
4. Thermostat setting.	Thermostat left on too cold a setting for too long a time. Turn to warmer setting.

Freezer short cycles

POSSIBLE CAUSES	WHAT TO TRY
1. Low voltage.	Test voltage at wall outlet with a voltmeter. This should be within 10 percent of normal. Call power company if it's low.
2. High room temperature.	Lower the temperature or move the freezer to a cooler place.
3. Freezer overloaded with unfrozen food.	Add no more than 10 percent of freezer capacity at one time; remove some food or add dry ice.
4. Defective relay or overload protector.	See chart, "Compressor does not run."

Excessive current draw

POSSIBLE CAUSES	WHAT TO TRY
1. Door opened too often.	Limit number of door openings to keep air at room temperature out of the freezer.
2. Heavy warm-food loads.	Do not overload freezer. See manufacturer's instructions for correct freezer capacity; do not exceed it.
3. Thermostat set too low.	Move thermostat to warmer setting.

Noisy operation

POSSIBLE CAUSES	WHAT TO TRY
1. Freezer not level.	Level freezer.
2. Tubing vibrating.	Adjust tubing slightly so that it does not rub against cabinet.
3. Loose compressor mounting.	Tighten leg mountings of compressor.

Door does not open or close properly

POSSIBLE CAUSES	WHAT TO TRY
1. Freezer not level.	Level freezer.
2. Latch mechanism worn or out of adjustment.	Examine latch mechanism. If worn, replace it. If not, adjust it according to manufacturer's specifications.
3. Hinge mounting screws loose.	Realign and retighten mounting screws. Replace any worn bushings.
4. Door vacuum.	Normal. This occurs when there is a brief interval between door openings; inrush of air at room temperature contracts when cooled to create partial vacuum.

DEFROST THERMOSTAT

LIGHT AND FAN SWITCH

Causes of line restriction

A partial or complete restriction in a line interrupts the normal flow of refrigerant through the system. It may be caused by moisture frozen in the capillary tube, by wax resulting from a breakdown of oil in the compressor or particles of dirt or lacquer from compressor windings.

A partial restriction produces symptoms like those of an undercharged system, plus frost buildup between the restriction and the suction line. It may clear itself when the compressor shuts off but reappear when the compressor starts again.

With a complete restriction there is no refrigerant flow at all. Evaporator and condenser remain at room temperature, the compressor refuses to start and cycles on the overload protector.

Compressor problems

The compressor itself may be subject to shorting, grounding, jamming or open windings (it will hum with one open winding). Continuity tests, using the manufacturer's wiring diagram, can isolate these problems, but compressor repair or replacement should not be attempted by the homeowner.

Typical dryer components

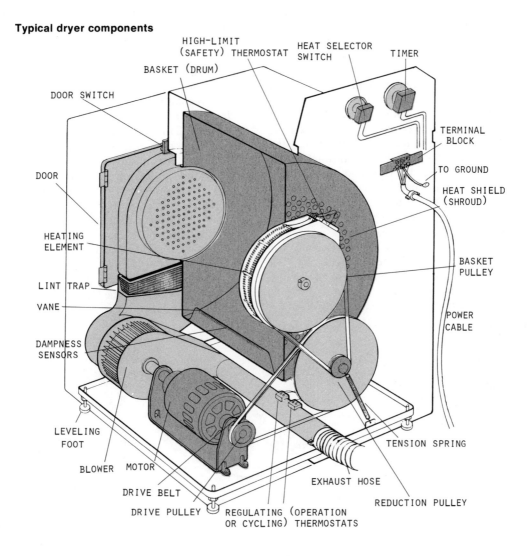

Electric dryer repair

■ AN AUTOMATIC CLOTHES DRYER is probably the simplest of major appliances: Basically, its function is to pass hot air across and through wet clothes to evaporate moisture from them.

The major components of an electric dryer are a basket to hold the clothes, fan or blower to move the air, motor to turn both basket and fan, resistance-wire heating element to heat the air, and controls for motor and heating element.

An electric dryer is normally run on a 30-amp., 220-v. circuit, with the heating element operating on a full 220 v. and the motor on 110 v. Some dryers are designed to run on 110-v. circuits as well. But, while this is perfectly safe, the heating element is less efficient at the lower voltage and drying time is considerably longer.

Nearly all electric dryers work like this: Air at room temperature is drawn into the appliance at the bottom or through front or rear openings. It is passed to the heating element, heated and drawn into the clothes basket. In dryers with un-shrouded baskets, hot air enters through holes at the rear of the basket; in dryers in which the basket is shrouded, hot air is drawn into the shroud and enters the basket through holes around its side. Passing over and through tumbling clothes in the basket, the hot air picks up moisture and lint (a result of normal wear) from them. When it leaves the basket at the front through ducting built into the door assembly, the air passes through a screen lint trap, usually just below the door. The air then is sucked into the blower, and forced through a duct to an exhaust hose that leads outdoors.

Motor and heating element are controlled by a

timer, a heat-selector switch, two or more thermostats, a door switch and, in newer machines, an electronic dampness sensor. The thermostat located near the heating element, called a high-limit thermostat, is a safety device and will not trip if the machine is operating normally. One or more regulating thermostats govern the heating element in normal operation. In old dryers, these may be of the adjustable, capillary type (you should *not* attempt to adjust one of these). Simple bimetal thermostats are more common. Regulating thermostats are usually located in the door assembly or on the exhaust duct, one for each heat setting for which the dryer is designed.

A dryer with a permanent-press cycle may have a "cool-off" regulating thermostat to run the motor with heat off until clothes cool to about 115°F.

Operation of electronic dampness sensors is based on the fact that the electrical resistance of clothing increases as it dries. Damp clothes

TIMERS

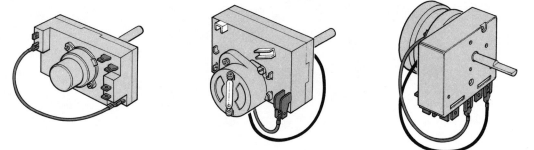

Motor does not start

POSSIBLE CAUSES	WHAT TO TRY
1. Line fuse blown.	Replace fuse (or reset circuit breaker).
2. Door open.	Close door tightly.
3. Timer defective.	Check the line voltage at timer. Turn timer on and place 115-v. test lamp across its terminals. If you get a reading, it indicates open contacts. Replace contacts or timer.
4. Door switch defective.	Remove wires from door switch, place continuity tester across terminals and press button. No reading indicates a defective switch. Replace.
5. Motor wiring loose or disconnected.	Tighten or reconnect loose or disconnected wires.
6. Centrifugal switch defective.	Refer to the manufacturer's schematic diagram for switch terminals on the motor; place continuity tester across terminals. If you get no reading, replace switch or motor.
7. Motor defective.	Direct-test motor with test jumper. If motor still fails to run, replace.

DOOR SWITCHES

Motor hums

POSSIBLE CAUSES	WHAT TO TRY
1. Voltage too high or too low.	Check panel fuses or circuit breakers. Check voltage at dryer line or terminals. Any variation greater than 15 percent from normal can cause hum. Notify power company.
2. Centrifugal switch in motor stuck.	Remove both motor and switch. Grease shaft, clean the contacts and reassemble. If the switch still sticks, replace it.
3. Basket binding or idler wheel broken.	Check the basket while turning it by hand. Replace any worn or broken idler wheels. Check leveling of machine.
4. Motor defective.	Direct-test motor with test jumper. Replace it if it fails to operate properly.

MOTOR AND MOUNT

THERMOSTATS

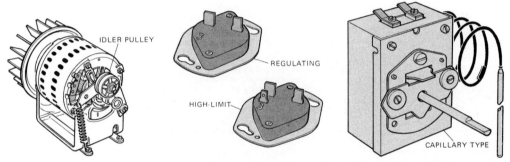

Motor hums, basket does not rotate

POSSIBLE CAUSES	WHAT TO TRY
1. Broken belt.	Remove back of dryer and replace any broken belts you find.
2. Loose pulley.	Check setscrews in all pulleys. If pulleys are slipping on their shafts, realign them first and then tighten setscrews.
3. Tension spring broken.	Replace broken tension spring.
4. Basket binding or idler wheel broken.	Check the basket while turning it by hand. Replace any worn or broken idler wheels. Check leveling of machine.

BASKET DRIVE WITH REDUCTION PULLEY

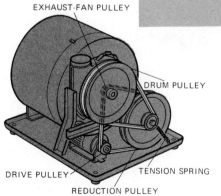

Noisy operation

POSSIBLE CAUSES	WHAT TO TRY
1. Loose fan.	Retighten fan-blade setscrew on motor shaft.
2. Loose objects caught in basket.	Remove all loose objects from basket.
3. Loose motor pulley.	Retighten motor-pulley setscrew.
4. Worn belt.	Replace any worn or frayed belts.
5. Basket binding.	Turn basket by hand to locate the point of binding. Check felt gaskets, wire harnesses and leveling of the unit.
6. Vibration.	Check for a loose fan blade, an out-of-balance fan blade, also for worn basket bearings and motor mounts. Tighten any loosened parts and replace worn parts.

QUICK corrective action when the dryer runs noisily is the best insurance against more serious damage to the dryer later.

Clothes dry slowly or not at all

POSSIBLE CAUSES	WHAT TO TRY
1. Drum overloaded.	Check size of load. Refer to the manufacturer's minimum and maximum standards.
2. Operating thermostat defective.	Place a thermometer in an exhaust duct, then record the temperatures at which the dryer heat is turned on and off. Check these figures against the manufacturer's specifications. If they should be out of the suggested range, replace the thermostat.
3. Lint trap clogged.	Clean lint trap thoroughly.
4. Heating element open.	Place a continuity tester across the heating-element terminals. If there is no reading, an open coil is indicated. Replace.
5. Exhaust hose clogged.	Clear exhaust hose.
6. Timer set too low.	Check your owner's operating manual; then increase the timer setting.
7. Blown panel fuse or tripped circuit breaker.	Check fuse or circuit breaker at the panel; then replace or reset it. If fuse or breaker should blow or trip again, then check for a short circuit in the heating element.
8. 110-v. operation.	If possible, change to 220-v. operation. Clothes takes 2½ to 3 times longer to dry on 110-v. line.
9. Clothes excessively wet when placed in the dryer.	See that clothes are spun-dry or wrung out—not dripping wet—before they are placed in dryer.

TOO OFTEN, slow drying will occur because the maker's instructions are not followed to the letter. The first step is to reread the operating instructions.

complete a circuit across sensor elements located on or near the basket vanes. By measuring their resistance in this circuit, the sensor determines whether or not a desired dryness has been reached, and shuts off the dryer when it has. Repair of these sophisticated electronic controls should also be turned over to a qualified serviceman.

A dryer basket may be driven by a belt that passes around it and also passes over a pulley on the motor shaft. Where the dryer is equipped with a shrouded basket, that basket is usually driven through two belts and a reduction pulley.

A dryer motor has two windings—one for starting and one for running. It is shifted from the former to the latter winding by a centrifugal switch. The motor terminals and their corre-sponding wires are usually coded with matching colors. Refer to the manufacturer's schematic diagram for correct terminals when you test your equipment.

The troubleshooting charts on these pages should help you correct most common electric dryer problems. Gas dryers are discussed in another article. When working on your electric dryer, or any other appliance, follow these safety precautions:

■ Refer to your manufacturer's manual to locate components.

■ Be sure that power is *turned off* before you handle components.

■ Make all of your continuity tests with *power off.*

■ When making tests with a 115-v. lamp, turn

DRYER ASSEMBLY

AIRFLOW PATTERN IN TYPICAL DRYER

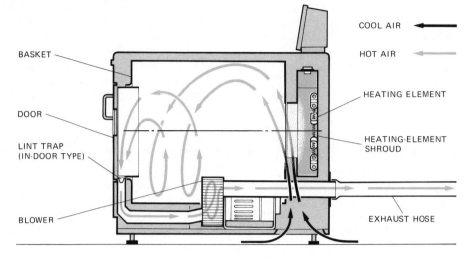

BASKET

DOOR

LINT TRAP
(IN-DOOR TYPE)

BLOWER

COOL AIR ◀━━━

HOT AIR ◀━━━

HEATING ELEMENT

HEATING-ELEMENT
SHROUD

EXHAUST HOSE

Dryer does not shut off

POSSIBLE CAUSES	WHAT TO TRY
1. Timer defective.	Check for a stuck timer or welded contact points. Replace.
2. Door switch defective.	Remove wires from the door-switch terminals; then place continuity tester across terminals. If there is a reading before the switch button is pressed, replace.
3. Operating thermostat defective.	Check thermostat against the manufacturer's specifications with a thermometer in the exhaust duct. If defective, replace.
4. Motor grounded.	Remove wires from motor terminals. Touch one lead of the continuity tester to a terminal and the other lead to the motor housing. If you get a reading on the tester, the motor is grounded. Replace.

power off first, connect the lamp, turn power on again, observe the result, then turn power off again and disconnect the lamp.

■ Make sure that the appliance is properly grounded, in accordance with your local electrical code.

■ Use replacement parts that meet factory specifications; those that are made by the manufacturer of the appliance are your best bet.

Extra tips: Before replacing an electrical part you believe to be faulty, make sure that the problem isn't caused by a loose connection. Tighten all connections after replacing an electrical part. Use new parts, not rebuilt ones, unless your appliance is so old that you can expect little further service from it.

Gas dryer repair

■ A GAS CLOTHES DRYER, like an electric dryer, is designed to remove moisture from damp clothes by passing hot air over and through them. In place of a simple heating element, a gas dryer has a burner with complex controls and safety devices. While controls and ignition systems vary from one manufacturer to another, there are a few basic types and troubleshooting charts on the following pages will tell you how to deal with the most common problems that may

arise. Gas problems more complicated than those covered in the charts should be handled only by a qualified service professional

Many electrical and mechanical functions of a gas dryer are the same as those of an electric model and many of its problems are handled the same way—these are also covered in the charts. But the electronic dampness sensors found on many newer gas and electric dryers are delicate devices best left to the professional

Typical gas dryer components

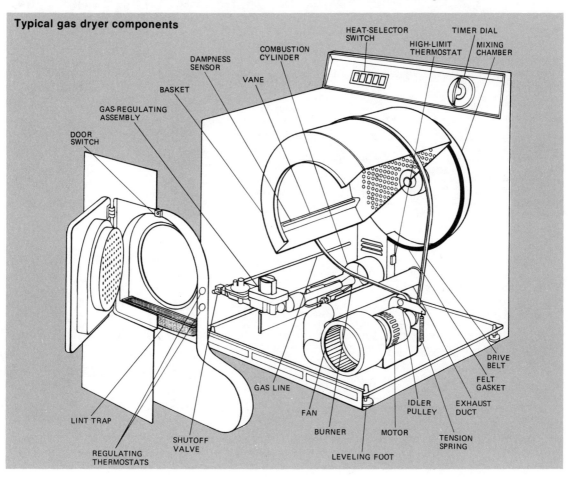

Motor does not start

POSSIBLE CAUSES	WHAT TO TRY
1. Fuse blown.	Replace fuse (or reset circuit breaker).
2. Door open.	Close door tightly.
3. Timer defective.	Check the line voltage at timer. Turn timer on and place 115-v. test lamp across its terminals. If you get a reading, it indicates open contacts. Replace contacts or timer.
4. Door switch defective.	Remove wires from the door switch, then place continuity tester across the switch terminals and press button. No reading indicates a defective switch. Replace.
5. Motor wiring loose or disconnected.	Tighten or reconnect loose or disconnected wires.
6. Centrifugal switch defective.	Refer to the manufacturer's schematic diagram for switch terminals on the motor; place continuity tester across terminals. If you get no reading, replace switch or motor.
7. Motor defective.	Direct-test motor with test jumper. If motor still fails to run, replace.

DOOR SWITCH

Motor hums

POSSIBLE CAUSES	WHAT TO TRY
1. Centrifugal switch in motor stuck.	Remove both motor and switch. Grease the shaft, clean the contacts and reassemble. If the switch still sticks, replace it.
2. Basket binding or idler wheel broken.	Check the basket while turning it by hand. Replace any worn or broken idler wheels. Check leveling of machine.
3. Motor defective.	Direct-test motor with test jumper. Replace motor if it fails to operate properly.

TIMER

Motor runs, basket does not rotate

POSSIBLE CAUSES	WHAT TO TRY
1. Broken belt.	Remove back of dryer and replace any broken belts you find.
2. Loose pulley.	Check setscrews in all pulleys. If pulleys are slipping on their shafts, realign them first and then tighten setscrews.
3. Tension spring broken.	Replace broken tension spring.
4. Basket binding or idler wheel broken.	Check the basket while turning it by hand. Replace any worn or broken idler wheels. Check leveling of machine.

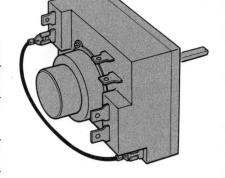

Noisy operation

POSSIBLE CAUSES	WHAT TO TRY
1. Loose fan.	Retighten fan-blade setscrew on motor shaft.
2. Loose objects caught in basket.	Remove all loose objects from basket.
3. Loose motor pulley.	Retighten motor-pulley setscrew.
4. Worn belt.	Replace any worn or frayed belts.
5. Basket binding.	Turn basket by hand to locate the point of binding. Check felt gaskets, wire harnesses and leveling of the unit.
6. Vibration.	Check for a loose fan blade, an out-of-balance fan blade, also for worn basket bearings and motor mounts. Tighten any loosened parts and replace worn parts.

TIMER

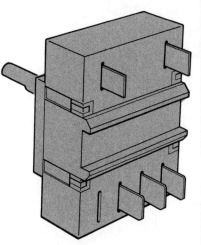

Dryer does not shut off

POSSIBLE CAUSES	WHAT TO TRY
1. Timer defective.	Check for a stuck timer or welded contact points. Replace.
2. Door switch defective.	Remove wires from the door-switch terminals; then place continuity tester across terminals. If there is a reading before the switch button is pressed, replace switch.
3. Operating thermo-stat defective.	Check thermostat against the manufacturer's specifications with a thermometer in the exhaust duct. If defective, replace.
4. Motor grounded.	Remove wires from motor terminals. Touch one lead of the continuity tester to a terminal and the other lead to the motor housing. If you get a reading on the tester, the motor is grounded. Replace.

PATTERN OF AIRFLOW in most gas dryers is shown below—air is mixed with hot flue products behind basket, sucked through it and through lint trap to fan; then it's forced out through exhaust duct and hose. Below, right, is the type of basket-drive system generally found in the dryers that do not use the single-belt drive.

AIRFLOW IN DRYER

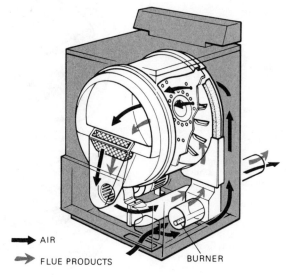

→ AIR

→ FLUE PRODUCTS

BURNER

BASKET DRIVE WITH REDUCTION PULLEY

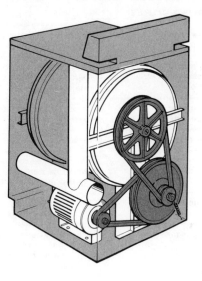

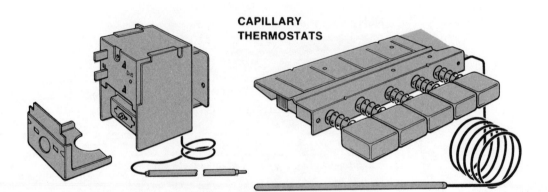

CAPILLARY THERMOSTATS

Clothes dry slowly or not at all

POSSIBLE CAUSES	WHAT TO TRY
1. Basket overloaded.	Check size of load. Refer to manufacturer's minimum and maximum standards.
2. Operating thermostat defective.	Check thermostat against the manufacturer's specifications with a thermostat in the exhaust duct. Replace thermostat if it does not operate at correct temperatures.
3. Lint trap clogged.	Clean lint trap thoroughly.
4. Exhaust hose clogged.	Clear exhaust hose.
5. Main burner orifice too small.	Check size of orifice (usually stamped on fitting) against manufacturer's specifications. Replace if incorrect.
6. Timer set too low.	Check owner's operating manual and increase the timer setting.
7. Ignition assembly defective.	Refer to following charts that cover pilot and ignition problems.

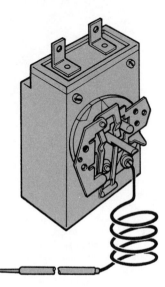

BIMETAL THERMOSTATS

Pilot will not light or goes out

POSSIBLE CAUSES	WHAT TO TRY
1. Loose connections in thermocouple circuit.	Check thermocouple fittings and tightness of screws on terminal leads.
2. Vent pipe off fan housing; draft blows pilot out.	Check position of the vent pipe (exhaust duct). Reposition it if necessary and secure it with a retaining clip.
3. Pilot burner or orifice dirty.	Check and clean pilot burner and orifice. Do not ream orifice.
4. Filter clogged.	Clean or replace pilot line filter.
5. Thermocouple defective.	Check thermocouple voltage with pilot on. Reading should be between 10 and 18 millivolts. Check against manufacturer's specifications.
6. Magnetic (Baso) valve defective.	Check thermocouple voltage as above. If okay, replace Baso valve.
7. Low gas pressure.	Pressure after regulator should be 2 to 3 ounces per square inch, or show a 3½-in. water column in a U-tube manometer, with the main burner operating. Check with gas company if low.

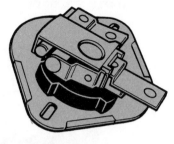

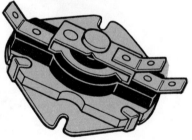

Pilot lights, main burner does not light

POSSIBLE CAUSES	WHAT TO TRY
1. Orifice plugged.	Clean main burner orifice.
2. Main solenoid coil defective.	Disconnect power and remove leads from solenoid coil. Place continuity tester across terminals. No reading indicates a defective or open solenoid. Replace.
3. Open circuit to main solenoid.	Disconnect power. Check continuity of circuit through pilot switch, door switch, thermostats and line fuse. Correct wherever circuit is open.
4. Timer defective.	Turn timer on. Check voltage at the solenoid with 115-v. test lamp. No voltage indicates a defective timer. Replace.
5. Valve closed.	Open valve in line to main burner.
6. Centrifugal switch in motor defective.	See "Centrifugal switch defective" in chart titled "Motor does not start"

CAUTION: Be sure power is turned *off* before you handle components. Make all continuity tests with power *off*. When using a test lamp, keep power *off* while connecting and disconnecting the lamp. Use your manufacturer's manual to locate components, and use only replacement parts that meet his specifications.

MANUAL-IGNITION BURNER ASSEMBLY

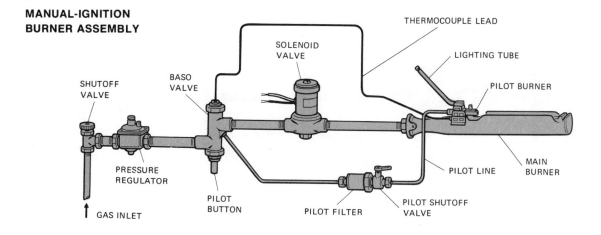

MANUAL-IGNITION BURNER

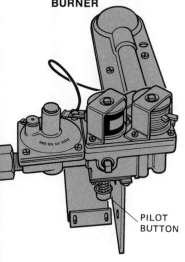

Pilot burning high, low or erratically

POSSIBLE CAUSES	WHAT TO TRY
1. Orifice clogged.	Clean orifice—do not ream.
2. Pilot out of adjustment.	Adjust pilot by means of screw on Baso valve to raise or lower flame.
3. Orifice wrong size.	Check orifice size against the manufacturer's specifications. Replace if wrong.
4. Filter clogged.	Clean or replace pilot line filter.
5. Gas pressure too high or too low.	See "Low gas pressure" in preceding chart.
6. Yellow-tipped flame.	Open air shutter or use smaller orifice. Clean orifice—do not ream.
7. Orange flame.	Clean orifice, surrounding area—do not ream.

Glow coil does not heat

POSSIBLE CAUSES	WHAT TO TRY
1. Broken or damaged coil.	Replace coil.
2. Leads broken or shorted to housing.	Replace broken leads; remove leads from shorted points. Check transformer secondary voltage.
3. Open circuit in transformer.	Disconnect power and check transformer windings for continuity. If open, replace transformer.
4. Open circuit between timer and transformer.	Disconnect power; check continuity through warp-switch (bimetal) contacts, fuses, safety pilot contacts, timer contacts. Correct wherever open.

ELECTRIC-IGNITION ASSEMBLY

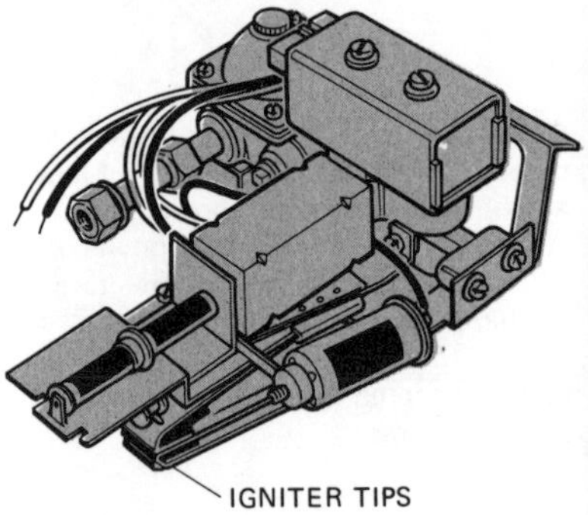

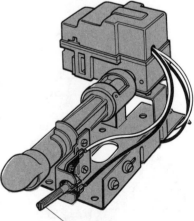

IGNITER TIPS

GLOW-COIL ASSEMBLY WITH PILOT

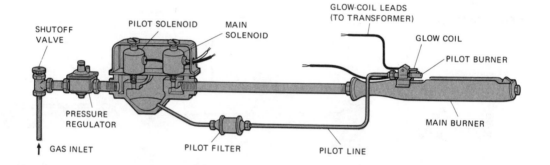

SHUTOFF VALVE

PILOT SOLENOID

MAIN SOLENOID

GLOW-COIL LEADS (TO TRANSFORMER)

GLOW COIL

PILOT BURNER

PRESSURE REGULATOR

MAIN BURNER

GAS INLET

PILOT FILTER

PILOT LINE

Glow coil heats, pilot does not ignite

POSSIBLE CAUSES	WHAT TO TRY
1. Orifice plugged.	Clean pilot orifice—do not ream.
2. Valve shut.	Open gas valve.
3. Pilot solenoid defective.	Disconnect power and solenoid leads. Test for continuity across terminals. No reading indicates a defective solenoid. Replace.
4. Vent pipe off fan housing causing draft across pilot.	Check position of the vent pipe (exhaust duct). Reposition it if necessary and secure it with a retaining clip.
5. Coil not hot enough.	Glow coil should be white hot. Refer to the following chart.

GLOW-COIL BURNER ASSEMBLY

GLOW COIL

Glow coil not hot enough

POSSIBLE CAUSES	WHAT TO TRY
1. Loose connection or short circuit.	Check and tighten all connections in the circuit. Reposition leads to avoid shorting them to bracket or housing.
2. Low voltage.	Check the line voltage, then check the voltage on both sides of the transformer against the manufacturer's specifications. If low, replace the transformer.

Automatic washer repair

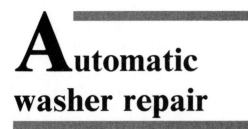

■ A MALFUNCTION in your automatic washer usually affects a basic function: fill, wash (agitation), drain or spin.

The troubleshooting charts on these pages will help you pinpoint a problem and correct it. To determine what the common components look like and their location, refer to the large illustration. It's a composite that's typical of most machines.

COMMON WASHER COMPONENTS

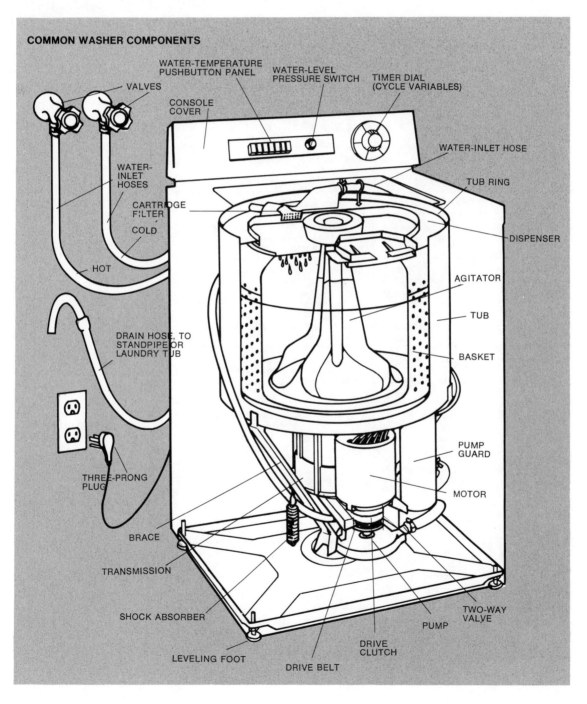

VALVES

WATER-TEMPERATURE PUSHBUTTON PANEL

WATER-LEVEL PRESSURE SWITCH

TIMER DIAL (CYCLE VARIABLES)

CONSOLE COVER

WATER-INLET HOSE

WATER-INLET HOSES

TUB RING

CARTRIDGE FILTER

DISPENSER

COLD

AGITATOR

HOT

TUB

DRAIN HOSE, TO STANDPIPE OR LAUNDRY TUB

BASKET

PUMP GUARD

MOTOR

THREE-PRONG PLUG

BRACE

TRANSMISSION

SHOCK ABSORBER

TWO-WAY VALVE

LEVELING FOOT

DRIVE BELT

DRIVE CLUTCH

PUMP

When testing electrical components, consult your machine's wiring diagram, which is glued on the back of, or inside, the machine. The chart with this article will help you interpret the electrical symbols.

To test the timer, turn the control knob slowly from the "Off" position before the regular cycle to the spot in the cycle where the machine isn't working properly as you count the number of increments (clicks). Count the corresponding increments on the timer cam chart and determine which terminals should be closed. Timer contact terminals are marked on the timer and timer cam chart by a letter or numerical code. Connect a 115-v. test light to the terminals and turn on the machine. If the test light fails to light, the timer is faulty in that model and should be replaced.

Washer doesn't fill

POSSIBLE CAUSES	WHAT TO TRY
1. Water faucet(s) closed.	Open faucet(s).
2. Water inlet hoses kinked.	Straighten hoses.
3. Clogged water valve screens.	Remove screens and flush out sediment.
4. Damaged water valve solenoid.	Remove leads and connect a 115-v. test light across terminals, turn on electricity and move control knob to "Fill." No light signifies a bad solenoid. Replace.
5. Defective timer.	Test as described in text above.
6. Defective water temperature switch.	Remove leads and connect a 115-v. test light across terminals, turn on electricity and move control knob to "Fill." No light signifies a bad solenoid. Replace.
7. Defective water-level pressure switch.	The switch normally has three terminals. With switch in "Fill" position there is contact between two of the terminals with the third terminal "open." Make sure you connect a 115-v. test light across the terminals affecting "Fill." Consult the wiring diagram. Turn on electricity and move control knob to "Fill." No light signifies a bad solenoid. Replace.
8. Water valve internal malfunction.	Disassemble water valve and check each part for damage, paying particular attention to the guide assembly and diaphragm. Replace the bad part, if possible. If not, replace the whole valve.
9. Open circuit.	Using the wiring diagram as a guide, probe each wire connection with a 115-v. test light to determine if defective wiring or a loose connection is causing the problem. Be sure control knob is at "Fill" position.

*After taking each "action," reconnect power and test operation, but be sure to pull plug from wall receptacle before continuing.

Washer doesn't drain

POSSIBLE CAUSES	WHAT TO TRY
1. Kinked drain hose; clogged drain.	Straighten hose; clear drain.
2. Broken or slipping drive belt.	Replace or tighten.
3. Defective timer and open circuit.	If the motor doesn't kick into "Drain," test timer as described in text above. Also check for open circuit. Be sure the control knob is set to "Drain" position.

WATER VALVE

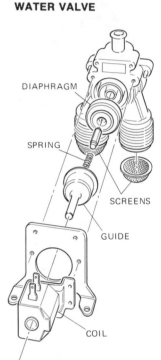

DIAPHRAGM

SPRING

SCREENS

GUIDE

COIL

WATER PUMP

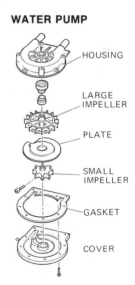

HOUSING

LARGE IMPELLER

PLATE

SMALL IMPELLER

GASKET

COVER

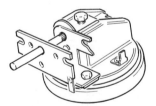

TIMER

WATER-TEMPERATURE SWITCH

WATER-LEVEL PRESSURE SWITCH

Washer doesn't agitate (wash)

POSSIBLE CAUSES	WHAT TO TRY
1. Broken or slipping drive belt.	Replace or tighten.
2. Defective drive clutch.	Remove the drive belt and turn the clutch by hand with the control knob in the "Wash" (agitate) position. If there is no "grab," the clutch is defective and should be replaced.
3. Defective transmission.	With the drive belt off, manually rotate the transmission pulley in agitate direction (usually clockwise) with control knob in "Wash" (agitate) position. If this doesn't drive the agitator, the problem is in the transmission.
4. Defective timer.	Test as described in text.
5. Faulty water-level pressure.	When water has filled the tub, contact reverts to the third terminal of this switch and to one of the other two terminals. The remaining terminal reverts to "Open" position. Make sure to connect a 115-v. test light across the terminals affecting "Filled." Consult the wiring diagram. Turn on the electricity and move the control knob to "Wash." No light signifies that you have a bad switch.
6. Open circuit.	Using the wiring diagram as a guide, probe each wire connection with a 115-v. test light to determine if either defective wiring or a loose connection is causing the problem. Make certain that the control knob is set at the "Wash" position.

Washer doesn't spin or spins slowly

POSSIBLE CAUSES	WHAT TO TRY
1. Broken or slipping drive belt.	Replace or tighten.
2. Loose motor pulley.	Tighten pulley.
3. Defective drive clutch.	Test as described under "Washer doesn't agitate," Cause 2 (above); be sure control knob is in "Spin" position.
4. Spin brake doesn't release or transmission is frozen.	The brake is not part of the transmission, but since they are attached and work together, they are checked as a unit. Set control knob in "Spin" position and remove drive belt. Turn brake stator; it should move freely. If not, the brake assembly or transmission is defective. Both units can be repaired.
5. Defective timer or open circuit.	If motor doesn't kick into "Spin," test timer as in text. Also check for open circuit. Be sure the control knob is set to the "Spin" position.

Abide by the following precautions:

• Be sure that electricity is turned off before handling components.
• Turn off water when working on water-handling components, such as the water valve.

• Before replacing an electrical component you believe is faulty, make certain that a loose connection isn't causing the problem.

• After replacing an electrical component, tighten connections.

• Before reconnecting your electrical service, see to it that ground wires are tightly attached.
• Make sure that water connections are secure.
• Install replacement parts that meet factory specification. You can't go wrong using parts made by the manufacturer of the washer.

Motor doesn't run

POSSIBLE CAUSES	WHAT TO TRY
1. Electrical service cord isn't plugged in; blown fuse or a tripped circuit breaker; possible malfunction in branch circuit.	Be sure that plug is connected and fuse or circuit breaker is okay. If there is no power at the wall receptacle, check the circuit.
2. Defective timer.	Test as described in text.
3. Defective lid switch.	Many models have a switch in the lid which automatically turns the washer off if door is open during cycling. If the machine refuses to operate with the lid closed, connect a test light across the lid switch. No light indicates a faulty switch. Replace.
4. Defective motor.	Most motors are protected by an internal overload circuit breaker that stops operation if the motor overheats. If this protective device halts motor operation, but the motor can be started again after about 30 minutes, consider the following conditions:

(a)
If the motor trips off when the machine goes into the spin cycle, the cause of trouble may be in the clutch, brake or transmission—not the motor. To find out, remove transmission drive belts and let the motor operate. If it doesn't trip off now, there is no motor problem.

(b)
If the motor operates in agitate position, but won't operate in spin position or vice versa, check timer and lid switch, and look for broken wire before condemning the motor.

5. Open circuit.	This possibility always exists, so before you rip the motor out of the machine conduct continuity tests with your test light at each wire connection.

*After taking each "action," reconnect power and test operation, but be sure to pull plug from wall receptacle before continuing.

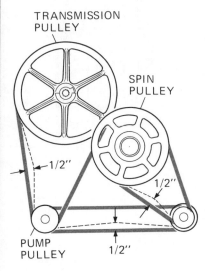

TRANSMISSION PULLEY

SPIN PULLEY

1/2"

1/2"

PUMP PULLEY

1/2"

PROPER belt tension is reached when you can deflect it ½ in. Minimum belt tension after extended use should be 15 pounds. To check this, hook spring scale at mid-point and note what force is required to deflect the belt 1 in.

Symbols found in wiring diagrams

ITEM	OLD	NEW	ITEM	OLD	NEW	ITEM	OLD	NEW
Ballast			Terminal			Double-throw thermostat		
Adj. Thermostat			Timer motor			Internal conductor		
Thermocouple			Plug connector			Harness wire		
Neon light	None		Starter (automatic)			Permanent connection		
Transformer	None		Light (incandescent)			3-prong plug		
Thermistor	None		Pressure sw.			Timer sw.		
Transistor	None		Fluorescent			Automatic sw.		
Diode (rectifier)	None		Coil			Manual sw.		
Rectifier (controlled)	None		Capacitor			Double throw		
Coil and switches			Resistor	500	500 Ω	Crossover		
Motor, single speed			Centrifugal sw.			Heater (wattage shown)	2800	2800w.
Motor, multispeed	1725 1140	1725 1140	Thermostat			Ground		

Dishwasher repair

■ WHEN DISHWASHER TROUBLES occur, they are most often caused by washing conditions—water problems, detergent problems, improper stacking of dishes or a combination of these factors. The accompanying trouble-shooting charts will help you correct these conditions, as well as common problems of mechanical origin. The illustration on the following page shows the typical locations of dishwasher components.

PROPER STACKING OF DISHES

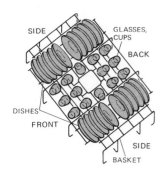

DOOR-LATCH ASSEMBLY

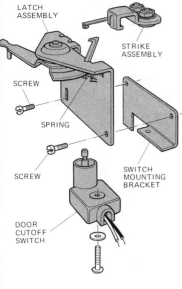

Machine does not operate

POSSIBLE CAUSES	WHAT TO TRY
1. Door not latched.	Latch door. Make sure handle locks all the way to the right.
2. Door microswitch defective.	Press button on microswitch manually. You should hear a definite clicking noise. If not, replace switch.
3. Latch lever or spring not pressing against microswitch.	Attach door latch to fully depress button or bend or replace spring on microswitch.
4. Timer defective.	Turn on the timer very slowly. It should advance and turn the machine on. If not, replace the timer.
5. Line wires loose or apart.	Check line junction box under machine. All wires should be tight and capped or taped.
6. Blown fuse or tripped circuit breaker.	Check fuse or circuit breaker.
7. Selector buttons not depressed fully.	Press desired cycle button all the way in.

Door will not close

POSSIBLE CAUSES	WHAT TO TRY
1. Door seal loose or binding inside tank.	Check entire door gasket. All gasket clips or points should be inserted in their proper slots.
2. Door striker.	Shim door striker until door latch catches it and closes very easily.
3. Improper installation.	Remove screw fasteners and let machine spring back, releasing it of any tension. Close door. If no binding, resecure screw fasteners in new position. Also, check level of machine.
4. Door hinges out of adjustment.	Check both hinges. If broken, replace. If out of adjustment, loosen hinge screws. Adjust door until it closes easily, then tighten screws.
5. Bottom service panel.	Check clearance of upper door with bottom service panel. If rubbing or binding, lower the panel or raise upper door by hinges.

The other illustrations show specific parts and assemblies from dishwashers made by several different manufacturers.

When making electrical checks and tests on a dishwasher or any other appliance, it is important to understand the manufacturer's wiring diagram. This diagram is shown in the instruction manual for portable dishwashers. For built-in models, the diagram can be found either be-hind the front-door panel or behind the control panel at the top of the door. It may be glued to the machine or rolled up. Since built-in dishwashers are wired directly to the main junction box, and because the combination of water and electricity can be lethal, it is important to use *extreme* caution when making any tests. Know what fuse or circuit breaker controls your dishwasher, and keep it *off* when working under the machine.

Common dishwasher components

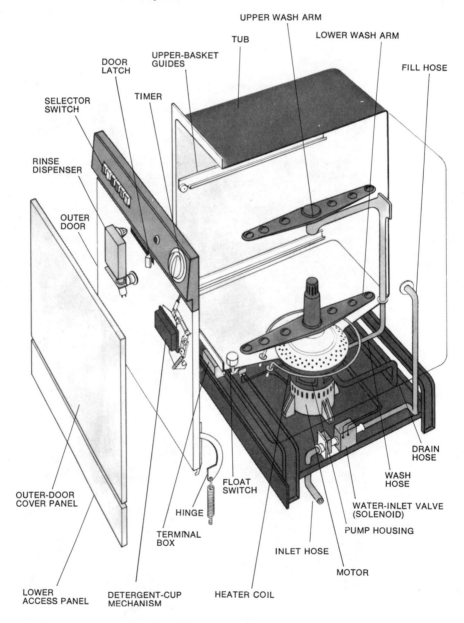

WASH MECHANISM

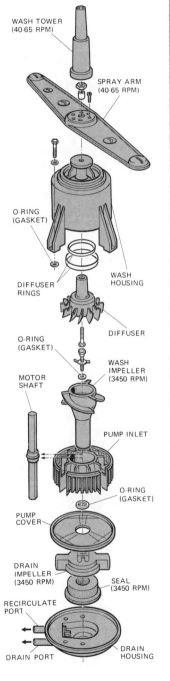

WASH TOWER
(40-65 RPM)

SPRAY ARM
(40-65 RPM)

O-RING
(GASKET)

DIFFUSER
RINGS

WASH
HOUSING

O-RING
(GASKET)

DIFFUSER

MOTOR
SHAFT

WASH
IMPELLER
(3450 RPM)

PUMP INLET

O-RING
(GASKET)

PUMP
COVER

DRAIN
IMPELLER
(3450 RPM)

SEAL
(3450 RPM)

RECIRCULATE
PORT

DRAIN PORT

DRAIN
HOUSING

Failure to fill

POSSIBLE CAUSES	WHAT TO TRY
1. Water valve solenoid.	Turn timer to fill position. Check voltage with 115-v. test light at terminals. If voltage exists but valve won't open, replace solenoid.
2. Water inlet line.	Be sure water valve is in full open position.
3. Float switch (some machines).	Check float-stem position on float switch. It should sit squarely in seat. To test, pick up float inside of tub and let it drop. Definite clicking noise should be heard. Check also for loose or fallen wire from float switch.
4. Pressure switch.	Press rubber diaphragm disc of switch with finger. Definite clicking noise should be heard. If not, replace pressure switch.
5. Water valve assembly.	Filter screen can be clogged. Disassemble and flush line and screen. Check calcium buildup near diaphragm and pin. Replace bad parts if possible. If not, replace whole valve.
6. Low water pressure.	Check flow pressure with screw-on gauge at sink. It must be between 15 and 120 p.s.i.

Water won't shut off

POSSIBLE CAUSES	WHAT TO TRY
1. Water valve stuck open.	Disassemble and clean. Check valve. If it still hangs up, replace.
2. Water-valve bleed hole clogged.	Disassemble valve and clean bleed hole in solenoid valve with pin.
3. Timer stuck on fill cycle.	Check timer. Fill cycle should last about 60 seconds. If timer doesn't advance, replace.
4. Float switch defective.	Check float switch for internal short. Place 115-v. test lamp across terminals. Depress switch spring; lamp should light. Release switch button; lamp should go out. If not, replace switch. Also, listen for definite clicking sound. If none, replace switch.

Dishwasher does not clean

POSSIBLE CAUSES	WHAT TO TRY
1. Not enough water.	See section on "Failure to fill" above.
2. Water not hot enough.	Check water temperature. It should be about 150° F. Run hot-water tap in sink before turning on machine or change temperature setting on house hot-water heater.
3. Wash or spray arm clogged.	Check holes in wash or spray arms for blockage by food particles or, possibly, small pieces of broken glass.
4. Not enough detergent or wrong kind.	Adjust detergent to correct water hardness. If water is hard, add more detergent. If detergent is caked in detergent dispenser cup, switch to a more granular brand.
5. Wash arm not turning.	Make sure that no utensil or dish is stopping wash-arm rotation.
6. Dishes improperly stacked.	Restack with space around each piece; avoid any clutter or pile-up. Face soiled sides of cups in top rack toward center of rack.

Water will not drain

POSSIBLE CAUSES	WHAT TO TRY
1. Pump impeller jammed or broken.	Check impeller blades for pieces of food jammed into them. Clear items and test. If impeller has broken vanes, replace.
2. Pump motor winding defective.	Advance timer to a drain cycle. If motor hums, check for obstacles in impeller. If impeller turns freely and motor still hums, then pump-motor winding is defective. Replace motor.
3. Drain hose kinked.	Check for any sharp bends in the drain hose. Straighten hose and place helical spring (tube bender), a little larger than the o.d. of hose, over kinked area to prevent a recurrence.
4. Drain hose clogged.	Disconnect drain hose from motor housing. Blow through the hose until line clears and reconnect it.
5. Timer stuck in wash cycle.	Check timer. If timer doesn't advance by itself, replace it.

Detergent cup fails to open

POSSIBLE CAUSES	WHAT TO TRY
1. Detergent left in cup too long, or put in a wet cup causing it to harden.	Use only amount of detergent specified by the manufacturer. Make sure cup is dry. If the detergent still cakes, switch to a more granular brand.
2. Improperly racked dishes or utensils.	Reposition around detergent cup all dishes or utensils that could possibly prevent the cup from opening.
3. White calcium deposits around cup. lid or shaft mechanism (due to hard water).	Clean all calcium deposits around mechanical operating mechanisms of the detergent. Use vinegar.
4. Detergent-cup solenoid valve.	Place 115-v. test lamp across both solenoid terminals. Advance timer in fill cycle until test light glows. If solenoid doesn't work, replace.
5. Timer.	Advance timer to positions in the fill cycle that activate detergent-cup mechanism. Place 115-v. test lamp across solenoid terminals. If no voltage is indicated, timer contacts are defective. Replace timer.

Motor will not run

POSSIBLE CAUSES	WHAT TO TRY
1. Motor hums.	Check for a food particle or piece of broken glass that's jammed in pump impeller. Clear and test.
2. Motor kicked out on overload.	Check line voltage, ±10 percent of 115 v., or binding of the motor shaft. Turn by hand to free shaft.
3. Timer defective.	Advance timer to all wash and drain cycles. Check motor operation on each one. If motor fails to run, replace timer.
4. Motor defective.	Direct-test motor with test jumper. If motor still fails to run, replace it.

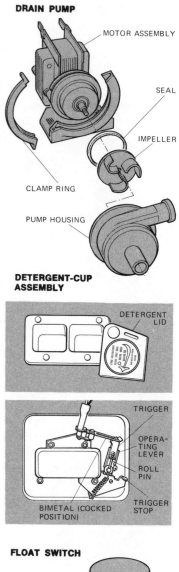

DRAIN PUMP

MOTOR ASSEMBLY

SEAL

IMPELLER

CLAMP RING

PUMP HOUSING

DETERGENT-CUP ASSEMBLY

DETERGENT LID

TRIGGER

OPERA-TING LEVER

ROLL PIN

TRIGGER STOP

BIMETAL (COCKED POSITION)

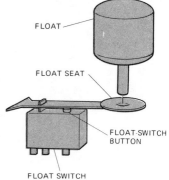

FLOAT SWITCH

FLOAT

FLOAT SEAT

FLOAT-SWITCH BUTTON

FLOAT SWITCH

Dishwasher operates when door is open

POSSIBLE CAUSES	WHAT TO TRY
1. Door switch is shorted.	Replace door switch.

Dishes do not dry

POSSIBLE CAUSES	WHAT TO TRY
1. Heater element burned out.	Replace heater element.
2. Calcium buildup on heater element.	Clean heater element of all calcium deposits.
3. Wire off heater element.	Replace wire and tighten connections.
4. Water not hot enough.	Check water temperature. It should be approximately 150° F.
5. Water still in dishwater.	Refer to section "Water will not drain."
6. Improper stacking of dishes.	Rack the dishes so that there is air space provided around each and see that they are neither jammed together nor piled on top of each other.
7. Fan motor inoperative (some machines).	Direct-test the fan motor with a test jumper wire. If the motor still fails to operate, replace it.

JUNCTION-BOX ASSEMBLY

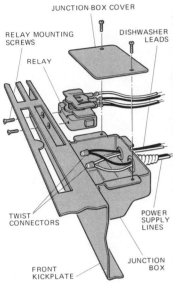

MAIN-DOOR ASSEMBLY

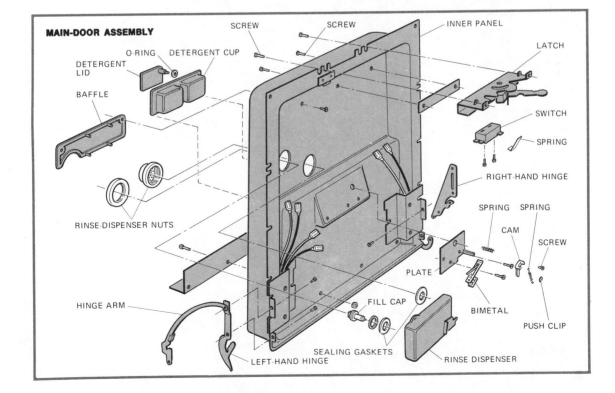

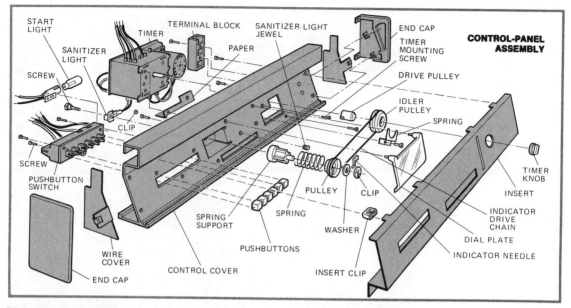

CONTROL-PANEL ASSEMBLY

(labels: START LIGHT, SANITIZER LIGHT, SCREW, TIMER, TERMINAL BLOCK, PAPER, SANITIZER-LIGHT JEWEL, END CAP, TIMER MOUNTING SCREW, DRIVE PULLEY, IDLER PULLEY, SPRING, CLIP, SCREW, PUSHBUTTON SWITCH, TIMER KNOB, INSERT, SPRING SUPPORT, SPRING, PULLEY, CLIP, WASHER, INDICATOR DRIVE CHAIN, DIAL PLATE, INDICATOR NEEDLE, WIRE COVER, END CAP, CONTROL COVER, PUSHBUTTONS, INSERT CLIP)

Dishwasher is leaking

POSSIBLE CAUSES	WHAT TO TRY
1. Door gasket loose or worn.	Check door gasket. It should be clipped in its proper slots. If gasket is torn or flat with no compression left, replace.
2. Door hinges broken or out of adjustment.	Replace broken hinges. Loosen hinges so door sits tight against gasket and retighten.
3. Inlet line fitting.	Check inlet line near water solenoid valve. Tighten compression nut.
4. Motor seal.	Check for water stains or leaks around motor shaft. Replace motor seal.
5. Door alignment.	Check door fit on gasket; it should not bind. See section "Door will not close."
6. Loose hose clamps.	Check all hoses and connections under machine for slippage or water stains.
7. Heating element seals.	Check seals at heating-element holes. If leaking, tighten. If leak remains, replace seals.
8. Nuts, bolts and screws.	Check attachments to tub. Noticeable dripping can be corrected by tightening or caulking the fasteners with putty.

Abnormal water noise

POSSIBLE CAUSES	WHAT TO TRY
1. Water hammer "thud noise."	Install water-hammer eliminator or pressure reducer (from maker) on inlet line to lower water pressure. Set water heater to 150° F.
2. Water chatter "low-frequency pulsing."	See that inlet piping is at least 3/8 in. i.d. Secure piping to avoid vibration. Set water heater to 150° F.
3. Water flutter "rumble."	Set water heater to 150° F. Install small hand valve in inlet line to cause partial restriction. If valve is already in line, close or open more to adjust pressure.
4. Water whistle "hiss" to shrill whistle.	See answer to No. 3 above and apply the same action.

WATER-INLET VALVE

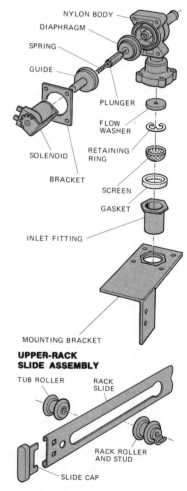

(labels: NYLON BODY, DIAPHRAGM, SPRING, GUIDE, PLUNGER, FLOW WASHER, RETAINING RING, SOLENOID, SCREEN, BRACKET, GASKET, INLET FITTING, MOUNTING BRACKET)

UPPER-RACK SLIDE ASSEMBLY

(labels: TUB ROLLER, RACK SLIDE, RACK ROLLER AND STUD, SLIDE CAP)

Dishwashing hints

POSSIBLE CAUSES	WHAT TO TRY
1. Water spots.	Too much detergent. Determine amount by experimentation. Use a rinse conditioner in the final rinse to eliminate water spots.
2. Stains and films.	Caused by water or household plumbing. Use oxalic acid, vinegar or Clorox to remove. Eliminate all silverware and metal to prevent their corrosion from this treatment.
3. Iron film (brown stain).	Wash dishes with full cup of detergent. Omit dry cycle. Use two teaspoons oxalic acid crystals. Wash dishes a second time. Eliminate dry cycle. Wash again with a full cup of detergent. Use dry cycle. Repeat precedure as necessary until stains are gone.
4. Lime film.	Too much detergent with very hard water. Use pint vinegar; run machine through cycle.
5. Coffee, tea and food stains.	Fill detergent cup. Pour 1 teaspoon liquid chlorine bleach over detergent. Operate the dishwasher through a normal cycle.
6. Metallic stains on dishes.	Aluminum abraded into a dish as a result of improper stacking. Remove with household alkali (Drano, lye, washing soda, Clorox).
7. Aluminumware discolored.	Rebrighten with cream of tartar. Fill detergent cup with cream of tartar and let dishwasher go through wash cycle only. Polish aluminumware with soap-filled steel wool pads.
8. Glasses and glassware filming and etching.	Water hardness causes glass to film. Eliminate it by using rinse agents, vinegar or citric acid. Etching cannot be eliminated.
9. Glass breakage.	Due to improper loading. Never wash glasses and cups in the lower rack; the force of water is enough to knock them together or blow them upward out of the rack completely.

RINSE DISPENSER

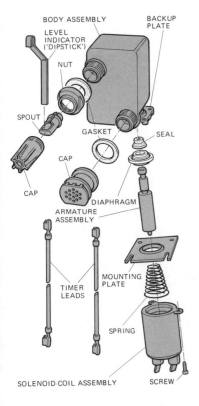

DOOR-HINGE ASSEMBLY

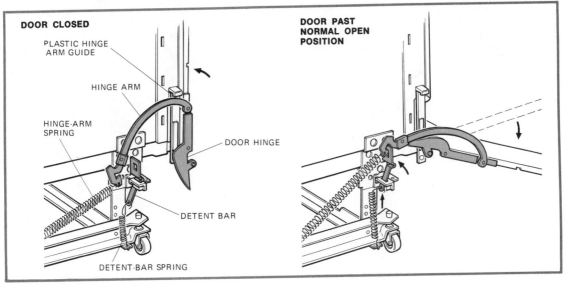

Water heater troubleshooting

■ IF YOUR WATER HEATER fails to perform satisfactorily, the fault may not lie within the heater at all. Leaking faucets or hot-water demands in excess of heater capacity may be the problem, or impure water may have damaged the heater and thus caused the trouble. The charts on the following pages will help you pinpoint and correct most common hot-water problems. The illustration shows the major parts of a typical electric water heater and their locations. Other illustrations show components made by different manufacturers, and gas-heater details.

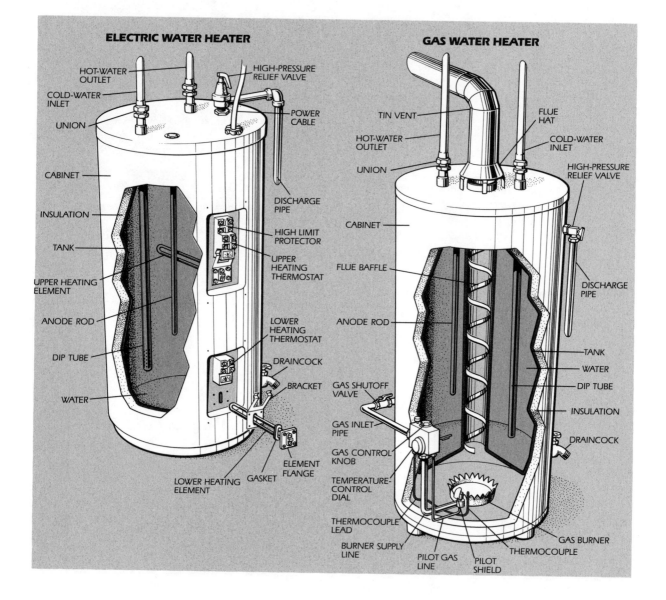

ELECTRIC WATER HEATER

- HOT-WATER OUTLET
- COLD-WATER INLET
- UNION
- CABINET
- INSULATION
- TANK
- UPPER HEATING ELEMENT
- ANODE ROD
- DIP TUBE
- WATER
- LOWER HEATING ELEMENT
- GASKET
- ELEMENT FLANGE
- BRACKET
- DRAINCOCK
- LOWER HEATING THERMOSTAT
- UPPER HEATING THERMOSTAT
- HIGH LIMIT PROTECTOR
- DISCHARGE PIPE
- POWER CABLE
- HIGH-PRESSURE RELIEF VALVE

GAS WATER HEATER

- TIN VENT
- HOT-WATER OUTLET
- UNION
- CABINET
- FLUE BAFFLE
- ANODE ROD
- GAS SHUTOFF VALVE
- GAS INLET PIPE
- GAS CONTROL KNOB
- TEMPERATURE-CONTROL DIAL
- THERMOCOUPLE LEAD
- BURNER SUPPLY LINE
- PILOT GAS LINE
- PILOT SHIELD
- GAS BURNER
- THERMOCOUPLE
- DRAINCOCK
- INSULATION
- DIP TUBE
- WATER
- TANK
- DISCHARGE PIPE
- HIGH-PRESSURE RELIEF VALVE
- COLD-WATER INLET
- FLUE HAT

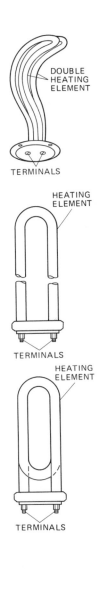

DOUBLE
HEATING
ELEMENT

TERMINALS

HEATING
ELEMENT

TERMINALS

HEATING
ELEMENT

TERMINALS

No hot water

POSSIBLE CAUSES	WHAT TO TRY
1. Blown fuse.	Replace fuse. If new fuse blows, a short circuit exists in water heater. Disconnect power. Remove panel and make visual inspection of wiring. If wiring is good, call service professional.
2. Heating element burned out.	Disconnect power. Place continuity tester across heating-element terminals. No reading indicates an open coil in element. Before replacing immersion-type element, close cold-water inlet valve and drain tank past element. Install new element. Refill tank, check for leaks and turn on power. On band heaters, loosen snap or bolt, slip band off tank and replace with new one. Retighten fasteners, replace insulation, turn on power.
3. Calcium buildup on heating element (immersion type).	Remove element. Use a vinegar-and-water solution to clean off all calcium deposits; then reinstall element.
4. Thermocouple defective (gas).	Clean pilot orifice. Turn thermostat valve to Pilot. Depress pilot button and light pilot. Hold button in for 30 to 40 seconds. If pilot fails to stay lit, replace thermocouple.
5. Thermostat defective (gas).	Turn thermostat valve to On position and temperature control to Hot position. Run hot water. If burner fails to light after two or three minutes, replace thermostat.

Typical gas water-heater controls

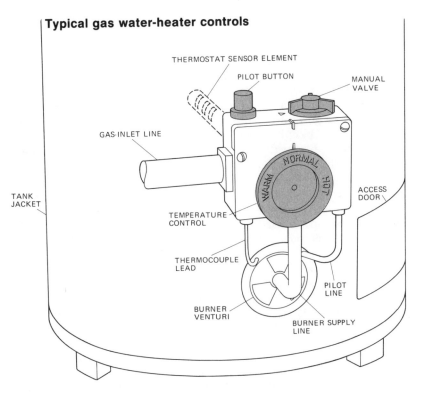

THERMOSTAT SENSOR ELEMENT

PILOT BUTTON

MANUAL VALVE

GAS-INLET LINE

ACCESS DOOR

TANK JACKET

TEMPERATURE CONTROL

THERMOCOUPLE LEAD

PILOT LINE

BURNER VENTURI

BURNER SUPPLY LINE

Not enough hot water

POSSIBLE CAUSES	WHAT TO TRY
1. Thermostat setting too low.	Turn setting to Normal (140°-150° F.)
2. Lower heating element burned out (immersion type).	Turn off power. Check element with continuity tester. No reading indicates an open coil. Replace.
3. Undersized tank.	Check quantity of water used by family and appliances. See hot water requirements chart.

Slow recovery between demands

POSSIBLE CAUSE	WHAT TO TRY
1. Top heating element burned out.	Turn off power. Check top heating element for continuity across terminals. If there is no reading, replace element.

Steam in hot water

POSSIBLE CAUSES	WHAT TO TRY
1. Thermostat contacts burned (electric).	Look for shorted or burned terminals. Replace thermostat.
2. Thermostat set too high.	Lower setting to Normal (140°-150° F.).
3. Thermostat runaway (gas).	Check whether thermostat is cutting off main burner. If burner fails to go out when temperature control is turned to Low, replace thermostat.

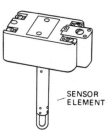

SENSOR ELEMENT

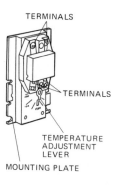

TERMINALS

TERMINALS

TEMPERATURE ADJUSTMENT LEVER

MOUNTING PLATE

A water heater is basically a storage tank. Cold water enters through the top and goes to the bottom through a pipe called a drop or dip tube. The water is heated by either electric elements or a gas (or oil-fired) burner rises to the top of the tank, and is discharged through the outlet pipe there. Thermostats are used to regulate the heat source in order to maintain a constant water temperature within the tank.

There are two types of electric water heaters, induction and immersion. An induction heater has a heating element strapped around the outside of the tank and covered with insulation. Heat passes through the wall of the tank to the water. In an immersion heater, the heating elements (usually two) pass through the tank wall directly into the water, with flanges and gaskets to keep the tank watertight where the elements enter. The wattage rating of the elements and the size of the tank will determine the time required for water to reach the desired temperature (recovery time). A large tank, holding more water than a small one, will also naturally require more electricity to heat a tankful of water.

Recovery time is the time a water heater takes to replace hot water. A minimum recovery rate would be eight hours to heat a tankful of 50° F. water to 150° F. This would allow the heater to recover overnight, so a family could start the day with a new tankful of hot water. For practical reasons, most water heaters sold today have a much quicker recovery rate than eight hours.

Any hot water that goes to waste will, of course, leave less hot water available to use. A leaking faucet is one of the most common forms of water waste. A slow drip—about one drop per second—wastes about 200 gal. of water a month, 5 tankfuls in the case of a 40-gal. heater. A more serious leak, such as a smooth stream that runs about 3 in. before breaking up into droplets, wastes about 1000 gal. a month. Other factors in hot-water waste are the amount of water standing in pipes and the number of running feet of pipe in the system; they should be taken into account when you plan any new water-heater installation.

There are two types of electric water heaters, induction and immersion. An induction heater has a heating element strapped around the outside of the tank and covered with insulation. Heat passes through the wall of the tank to the water. In an immersion heater, the heating elements (usually two) pass through the tank wall directly into the water, with flanges and gaskets to keep the tank watertight where the elements enter. The wattage rating of the elements and the size of the tank will determine the time required for water to reach the desired temperature (recovery time). A large tank, holding more water than a small one, will also naturally require more electricity to heat a tankful of water.

A typical two-element, electric water heater has a "load-limiting" circuit to keep both elements from drawing current at the same time. It operates as follows: With a tankful of cold water, the upper (secondary) heating element is turned on by the upper thermostat. About 25 percent of the total volume of water in the tank is heated by this element. The lower (primary) element is turned on only when the upper thermostat has sensed that the water at the top of the tank has reached the desired temperature and is ready for use. The lower element now heats the remainder of the water in the tank. If some of the hot water

High water-heating cost

POSSIBLE CAUSES	WHAT TO TRY
1. Leaking hot-water faucets.	Replace washers in all leaking faucets.
2. Thermostat setting too high.	Turn thermostat to Normal setting (140° to 150° F.).
3. Scale deposits appearing on heating elements.	Remove and clean elements. See "Not enough hot water."

Water under heater

POSSIBLE CAUSES	WHAT TO TRY
1. Thermostat leaking.	Check flange and gasket around thermostat. Replace gasket if leaking.
2. Plumbing connections.	Check all sweated (soldered) connections in and around tank. If leaks are found, make any necessary repairs.
3. Condensation.	Check for moisture buildup in insulation if basement is cold or damp. Moisture resulting from condensation will not drip steadily as it would from a leak.
4. Leak (hole) in tank.	Use boil plug for temporary repair if hole is accessible. Replace tank eventually.

Water black or discolored at faucets

POSSIBLE CAUSE	WHAT TO TRY
1. Magnesium in water.	Magnesium rod in tank is probably corroded. Shut off power and water supply. Remove metal band or screws from top panel of water heater. Remove insulation and then remove head of magnesium rod with socket wrench. Replace with a new rod, using sealer or Permatex on threads. Reassemble, turn on water and power. Allow about 24 hours for the lines to clear.

1 To prevent rust, dirt and condensation from entering the heater, install a dirt trap near the gas control valve. Make the drip leg from a short nipple and end cap.

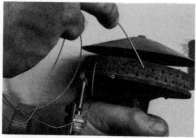

2 Slide a thin wire into the gas burner's openings to clear away rust and dirt deposits. Then, remove all surface rust from the burner's housing using a stiff wire brush.

3 Clean dirt from the pilot line and burner line to keep the heater operating smoothly. Remove the lines and push a thin wire through each line to dislodge dirt.

4 Remove the heater's thermocouple by loosening the screw on the retainer clip. Install the new thermocouple so that its heat sensor is in the path of the pilot flame.

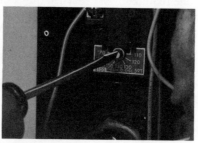

5 After installing a new thermostat, set the temperature indicator to 130° F. Wait about 45 minutes and then test the water temperature with a meat thermometer.

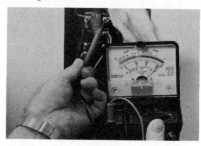

6 Use a voltage ohmmeter (VOM), as shown, to test the high-limit switch. Then, check the thermostat and elements. The VOM will detect a faulty component.

is used, cold water entering the tank through the drop tube is heated by the lower element. When all the water in the tank has been heated, the lower element is turned off by its thermostat. In the load-limiting circuit, wiring is usually color-coded with a blue lead to the upper element, a yellow lead to the upper thermostat and then to the upper element's other terminal, a red lead to the upper thermostat and then to the lower element and a black lead to the lower thermostat and then to the lower element's other terminal.

Gas water heaters have a single immersion thermostat, located near the bottom of the heater, a burner and a thermocouple-governed pilot light. Heater controls are a temperature dial, a pilot reset button and a manual valve with OFF, PILOT and ON positions. A thermocouple screwed into the base of the thermostat is attached to the burner and enveloped by the pilot flame. Gas from the main line enters the thermostat at one side.

The gas water heater is lit as follows: The pilot button is depressed, the pilot light is lit with a match or igniter, and the pilot button is held down for 30 to 45 seconds. The pilot flame striking the thermocouple head makes it generate a current that actuates a magnetic valve in the thermostat; this is a safety device that shuts off the supply of gas to the pilot light when it goes

out. The pilot button is released and the manual valve is turned to the ON position. The burner is now lit by the pilot light.

If the burner does not light, turn the temperature dial to a higher setting, then return it to NORMAL. The thermostat maintains a constant water temperature by means of a bimetal or bellows regulating the supply of gas to the burner.

With both types of water heater, a pressure-relief valve is installed in the cold-water line just above the tank. This valve gives protection from pressure buildup in case of thermostat failure. Most of these valves are set 25 to 35 pounds per square inch above normal water pressure, to a maximum of 125 p.s.i. Valves may be spring-operated and resettable or replaceable lead plugs that melt at high temperature.

Normal hot-water temperature is 140-150° F. Most water heaters also have temperature settings for WARM, about 120° F., and HOT, about 160° F.

Because water often contains corrosive impurities, water-heater tanks usually are made of copper and are glass lined. In addition, some heaters have a magnesium-rod anode. Corrosive agents will attack the rod instead of the tank, but when the rod has become badly corroded, it will discolor hot water and must be replaced.

Electric range troubleshooting

■ YOUR ELECTRIC RANGE is one of the simplest appliances in the house—it's really just heating elements and their controls. Although it uses 230-v. power, it's no more difficult to troubleshoot than a 115-v. appliance, so long as you show the respect you always should for the potential danger of electricity. And while the controls used on ranges have become increasingly sophisticated over the years, their basic principles have not changed.

Most electric ranges have four surface elements, two large ones and two smaller ones. The large elements can have a wattage of 2100 to 2600 w., while smaller ones range from 1150 to 1500 w. Older surface elements consisted of an open coil of wire fitted into a ceramic block.

Elements of this type are rarely seen today, except on hotplates, as they burn out easily. They have been replaced by hermetically sealed elements. This element has a Nichrome resistance wire embedded in an insulating powder, usually magnesium oxide, housed in D-shaped stainless-steel tubing. The insulating powder keeps the resistance wire from touching the tubing sheath.

A surface element has either one or two resistance elements and two or four connections. For these connections, one of three types of terminal—banana, knuckle or screw-on—is used. These terminal types are shown below. A terminal block used with the surface element provides a positive connection point between element and switch wiring. Terminal blocks are usually attached to the underside of the cooktop with a screw. Screw-on terminals have, instead of a terminal block, a glass or ceramic covering over terminal ends to prevent shorting. Problems that can arise with surface elements are shorting, breaks in Nichrome wire and pitted or corroded terminals; terminal blocks are also subject to corrosion and pitting, and to damage from internal arcing.

Surface switches are used to regulate the amount of heat produced by surface elements.

SURFACE-ELEMENT ASSEMBLY

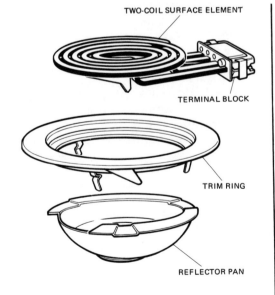

TWO-COIL SURFACE ELEMENT

TERMINAL BLOCK

TRIM RING

REFLECTOR PAN

SURFACE-ELEMENT CONNECTIONS

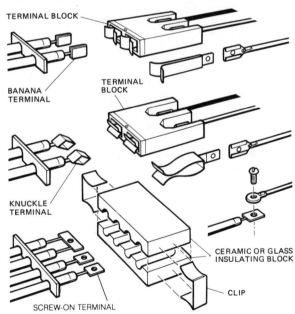

TERMINAL BLOCK

BANANA TERMINAL

TERMINAL BLOCK

KNUCKLE TERMINAL

CERAMIC OR GLASS INSULATING BLOCK

CLIP

SCREW-ON TERMINAL

The switches most commonly used are the step switch and the infinite-heat switch. The step type is a rotary or pushbutton switch that provides a choice of from five to seven different heats (wattages) by connecting the resistances in the surface element in parallel, in series, or singly to either 230-v. or 115-v. current. Typical wattages for a seven-heat switch could be 212, 287, 500, 850, 1150, 2000 and 3000.

The infinite-heat switch, which provides a continuous range of settings between "high" and "off," uses an internal bimetal strip, which is anchored at one end and has a switch contact at the other end. As current passes through the bimetal and heats it, it curls up and away from the cam-follower strip that carries the switch's other contact. The position of the cam determines how long the element will be on before the bending bimetal breaks contact and cycles the element off. In its extreme position—the "high" setting—the cam holds the contacts together without cycling.

Like surface switches, oven controls vary. Some ovens have only a thermostat, while others also have a selector switch and automatic clock. The selector switch is used where a range has more than one oven or there is more than one function for the thermostat to perform, or it can determine which oven elements are supplied with current and whether they are connected in series or in parallel.

The thermostat that regulates oven temperature has a fluid-filled sensing bulb, similar to the bulb at the end of a thermometer, suspended within the oven. Expansion of the fluid with increasing temperature activates a bellows in the thermostat that forces contacts apart, cutting off current to oven elements and cycling the oven off; reduced oven temperature and contraction of fluid bring the contacts together again, cycling the oven back on. The thermostat's control knob varies tension between contacts.

Checking oven thermostat

Thermostat calibration can be checked by putting a mercury (not bimetal) thermometer in the oven and setting the thermostat at 400° F. Let the oven cycle three or four times, then check the temperature; if it is more than 15° F. above or below the thermostat setting, the thermostat requires recalibration. Calibration instructions are usually stamped on the thermostat, but if none can be found, assume that a quarter turn equals 25° F. Turn the calibration screw in either direction, then observe the result. Check calibration annually, more often if the oven gets unusually heavy use.

Construction of oven elements is similar to that of surface elements. The broil element usually has two resistances, with a maximum 3000 w; the bake element is a single resistance rated at about 2500 w. Elements are fastened to the oven's rear wall, but can usually be lowered or lifted slightly.

A range clock may be fully automatic or nothing more than a clock with a buzzer timer. The fully automatic timer is connected to the oven controls.

Self-cleaning ovens

Electric self-cleaning ovens use temperatures of 850° to 1000° F. to decompose oven soil. The process, called pyrolysis, leaves only a loose ash that is easily removed. The self-cleaning oven has more insulation, heavier body metal, larger and more durable controls and a number of safety features.

The cleaning cycle uses the oven thermostat, a bias circuit and door-locking circuit. The bias circuit lets the thermostat run in the higher temperature range required for pyrolysis. The door-locking circuit assures positive locking of the oven door at temperatures over 550° F. and keeps the cleaning cycle from starting if the door is not locked; this circuit is essential for safety, as a rush of air mixing with carbonized soil at high temperature could cause an explosion.

The self-cleaning cycle also involves a cooling fan that circulates air in and around the oven liner and, usually, a smoke eliminator, a device that promotes the decomposition of smoke.

Setup sequence for cleaning and duration of cleaning vary among manufacturers. The appearance of the soil remaining at the end of a cleaning cycle indicates cleaning effectiveness. If it is brown and soft, no cleaning has taken place; if it is dark brown, cleaning has been incomplete. Loose gray ash indicates complete cleaning.

Continuous-cleaning ovens require none of the extra circuits and safety devices self-cleaning ovens do. They differ from ordinary noncleaning ovens only in the porcelain with which they are lined. This is somewhat porous, and allows fat spatters to spread out and then decompose at normal cooking temperatures.

THERMOSTAT COMPONENTS

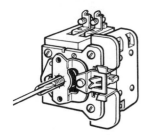

TEMPERATURE-SETTING KNOB
SPRING   PIVOT
BELLOWS
CONTACTS

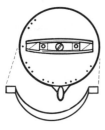

THERMOSTAT CALIBRATION POINTS

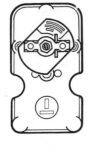

Oven does not heat

POSSIBLE CAUSES	WHAT TO TRY
1. Fuse blown or circuit breaker tripped.	Replace fuse or reset circuit breaker. If blowing or tripping is repeated, disconnect the power and check for shorts.
2. Automatic timer set improperly.	Make sure timer is in "manual" position for everyday cooking. Refer to manufacturer's instructions.
3. Automatic timer defective.	Check timer for defective motor or contacts (see clock-timer discussion.) If gears are bound or broken, repair or replace timer.
4. Selector switch set improperly.	Make sure that selector switch is set for type of cooking desired.
5. Thermostat defective.	Place voltmeter across thermostat input terminals; reading should be 230 v. Loosen bake element in oven and pull it forward a fraction of an inch to make terminals accessible; turn thermostat on and check voltage across bake-element terminals; reading should be 230 v. Otherwise, thermostat is defective and must be replaced. Check thermostat's broil operation the same way.
6. Element(s) defective.	Inspect bake and broil elements for breaks or cracks. Check elements one at a time as described above; if voltage is present but element does not heat, replace it.
7. Wires loose or shorted.	Disconnect power, check wiring for breaks or charring. Replace damaged wires. Be sure connections are tight.

Oven temperatures are uneven

POSSIBLE CAUSES	WHAT TO TRY
1. Thermostat out of calibration.	Check oven temperature with an accurate mercury thermometer. Recalibrate thermostat according to the maker's instructions.
2. Door gaskets defective.	Open oven door and inspect sealing gaskets; replace any that are worn, cracked or flat.
3. Door fit uneven.	Check door alignment; if adjustment is needed, loosen door-hinge screws, realign door, then retighten the screws. Check door springs, too; adjust for equal tension if necessary.

SEVEN-HEAT SWITCH OPERATION

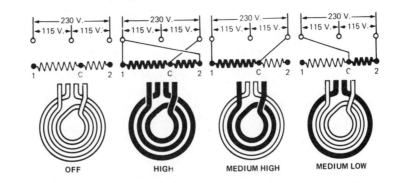

OFF   HIGH   MEDIUM HIGH   MEDIUM LOW

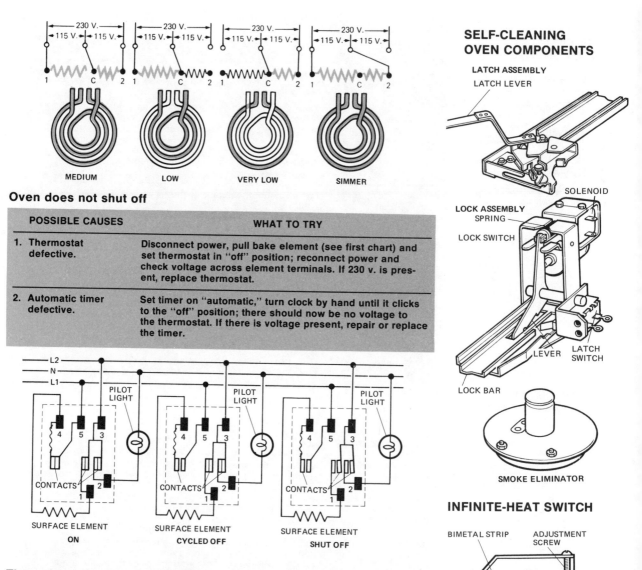

MEDIUM   LOW   VERY LOW   SIMMER

Oven does not shut off

POSSIBLE CAUSES	WHAT TO TRY
1. Thermostat defective.	Disconnect power, pull bake element (see first chart) and set thermostat in "off" position; reconnect power and check voltage across element terminals. If 230 v. is present, replace thermostat.
2. Automatic timer defective.	Set timer on "automatic," turn clock by hand until it clicks to the "off" position; there should now be no voltage to the thermostat. If there is voltage present, repair or replace the timer.

SURFACE ELEMENT
ON

SURFACE ELEMENT
CYCLED OFF

SURFACE ELEMENT
SHUT OFF

Timer does not operate properly

POSSIBLE CAUSES	WHAT TO TRY
1. Timer set incorrectly.	Refer to the manufacturer's instructions for correct settings.
2. Loose connection.	Disconnect power, tighten all loose connections, then reconnect power.
3. Motor defective.	Disconnect power, remove timer motor and test it directly with 115-v. power. If drive gear does not turn, replace the motor.
4. Blown fuse.	Inspect 15-amp. fuse behind control panel; replace if blown. If new fuse blows, disconnect power and check time for shorts (see clock-timer discussion.)
5. Gears worn, stripped or broken.	Inspect clock gears in timer; if any are visibly worn, broken or stripped, repair or replace timer. If gears are jammed, try to free them with silicone spray or a TV-tuner cleaner.
6. Contacts defective.	Make voltage checks on timer

SELF-CLEANING OVEN COMPONENTS

LATCH ASSEMBLY
LATCH LEVER
SOLENOID
LOCK ASSEMBLY
SPRING
LOCK SWITCH
LEVER
LATCH SWITCH
LOCK BAR

SMOKE ELIMINATOR

INFINITE-HEAT SWITCH

BIMETAL STRIP
ADJUSTMENT SCREW
FOLLOWER STRIP
CONTACTS
SHAFT
CAM

OVEN ELEMENTS

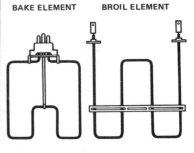

BAKE ELEMENT   BROIL ELEMENT

Surface unit does not heat

DOOR-HINGE ASSEMBLY

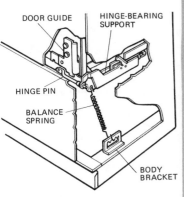

DOOR GUIDE

HINGE-BEARING SUPPORT

HINGE PIN

BALANCE SPRING

BODY BRACKET

POSSIBLE CAUSES	WHAT TO TRY
1. Fuse blown or circuit breaker.	Replace fuse or reset circuit breaker. If blowing or tripping is repeated, disconnect the power and check for shorts.
2. Connection loose or shorted.	Disconnect power, tighten any loose connections and replace any charred wiring, reconnect power.
3. Switch defective.	Place voltmeter across switch's input terminals (usually labeled L1 and L2); reading should be 230 v. Turn switch on and place voltmeter across output terminals (to surface element); reading should be 230 v. Replace switch if you do not get these readings.
4. Terminal block defective.	Disconnect power. Inspect inside of terminal block. If it is charred or broken, replace it. If it is pitted or dirty, try to clean it with a contact file; replace it if this cannot be done.
5. Surface element defective.	If element is the plug-in type, unplug it and then plug it into one of the sockets into which the element is known to work; if it does not heat there, replace it. If element is the screw-on type, pull it forward, turn switch on and place voltmeter across surface-element terminals; reading should be 230 v. If voltage is present and element does not heat, replace it. Any replacement element must be of same size and wattage as the original and have the same type of terminals.

Oven door drops down or pops open

FLUID SENSING BULB

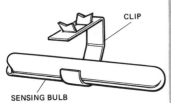

CLIP

SENSING BULB

POSSIBLE CAUSES	WHAT TO TRY
1. Door out of alignment.	Loosen door-hinge screws, realign door and retighten screws. Check to make sure range is level.
2. Hinge pin worn or loose.	Disassemble door, inspect hinge pins, replace them if worn or broken—an 8d nail can sometimes be used.
3. Hinge worn.	Hinge worn: replace hinge if edges are worn.
4. Spring broken.	Open door slightly. If it fails to spring closed or drops easily, a broken spring is likely. Inspect springs; if one is broken, replace both.
5. Roller bearing broken.	If door is hard to open or close, a bearing is broken. Replace both.

Oven drips water or sweats

POSSIBLE CAUSES	WHAT TO TRY
1. Oven preheated improperly.	Preheat oven with door open at first stop.
2. Oven temperature too high.	Use an accurate mercury thermometer to check on calibration of oven thermostat.
3. Door not sealing.	Check door alignment and condition of the door gaskets; realign door if necessary (see chart, "Oven temperatues are uneven.") Replace any worn, cracked or flat gaskets.
4. Oven vent clogged.	Inspect oven vents for obstructions and clear them. If the oven uses a filter clean or replace it.

Oven lamp does not light

POSSIBLE CAUSES	WHAT TO TRY
1. Bulb loose or defective.	Tighten bulb in socket. If it still does not work, replace it with a new *appliance* bulb.
2. Switch defective.	Disconnect power, disconnect both leads to switch, place a continuity tester across both switch leads and turn on the switch. There should be a reading of continuity. Turn the switch off. There should be no reading. Replace the switch if you do not get correct readings.
3. Bad contact in socket.	Disconnect power and remove bulb from socket. With finger or blade of a small screwdriver, bend the center socket contact outward a fraction of an inch. Replace bulb and reconnect power.

AUTOMATIC TIMER

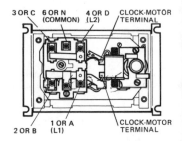

3 OR C 6 OR N (COMMON) 4 OR D (L2) CLOCK-MOTOR TERMINAL

2 OR B 1 OR A (L1) CLOCK-MOTOR TERMINAL

No heat for cleaning (self-cleaning ovens)

POSSIBLE CAUSES	WHAT TO TRY
1. Controls set improperly.	Refer to manufacturer's instructions for setting controls for cleaning cycle; after setting controls, wait a minute to determine whether they are working.
2. Fuse blown or circuit breaker tripped.	Replace fuse or reset circuit breaker; if blowing or tripping is repeated, disconnect the power, check for shorts.
3. Thermostat defective.	See chart "Oven does not heat."
4. Door unlocked.	Inspect door for firm seat against oven, make sure latch is all the way over in locked position; if not, check both door and locking mechanism for alignment.

TESTING AUTOMATIC TIMERS: Motor: voltage across terminals 1 and 6 should be 115; if not, check for blown 15-amp. fuse behind panel; if fuse is good, see whether motor drive wheel is turning; if not, replace motor. Switch: voltage across 1 and 4 should be 230, as across 2 and 3 with timer set on manual and when the timer has turned the oven on in automatic operation. If these voltage readings are not obtained, the timer must be repaired or replaced.

Cleaning is incomplete (self-cleaning ovens)

POSSIBLE CAUSES	WHAT TO TRY
1. Controls set improperly.	See chart "No heat for cleaning."
2. Cleaning time short.	See maker's instructions on length of cleaning time.
3. Oven elements defective.	See chart "Oven does not heat."
4. Line voltage low.	Check voltage at terminal block at rear of range; it should be within 10 percent of 230 v. If it is lower than 207 v., call local power company.
5. Smoke eliminator defective.	Disconnect power, locate smoke eliminator and disconnect its leads; then place continuity tester across eliminator terminals. Replace eliminator if there is no reading or if there are visible breaks in its mesh screen.

Garbage disposer troubleshooting

■ YOUR GARBAGE DISPOSER is a simple, reliable unit which should seldom give you any trouble unless you ask it to do things which it wasn't designed for. The first rule in maintaining your unit is to know exactly what should and should not be put into it. The instructions which came with it will tell you what you need to know.

Basically, there are two types of garbage disposers. The chief difference between the two types is the kind of motor each has. Less expensive models have a split-phase motor, while the costlier units have capacitor-start motors.

These motors are similar in most respects, but the capacitor-start motor has a capacitor which gives it an assist in starting—a substantial starting torque which allows it to handle heavier loads.

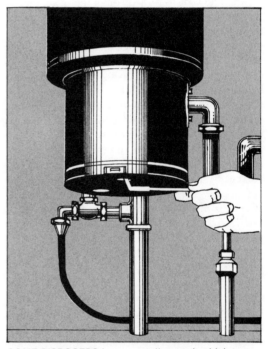

SOME DISPOSERS have a small wrench which can be inserted in the bottom to help free jam-ups. The wrench is used to turn the mechanism backwards.

All garbage disposers will grind and get rid of soft food wastes—meat particles, bread scraps, soft vegetable leftovers—but only those with capacitor-start motors have the muscle to grind seafood shells, bones, corncobs and other heavy food matter.

No garbage disposer is designed to handle non-food wastes. Don't try to grind glass, pottery, broken dishes, bottle caps, rubber, bits of metal or plastic. And keep silverware, paper, cardboard and even bits of string out of the unit. All of these items can damage the disposer and clog your drain.

BATCH-TYPE garbage disposers have a removable stopper, which must be inserted in the sink opening and turned to start the grinding action.

If you have heard those stories about grinding pop bottles in your disposer as a way of cleaning it, forget them. Broken bottles are bad, not good, for your unit.

Here are some good rules for getting the best and most trouble-free service from your disposer:

1. Grind only food wastes.

2. Follow the instructions which came with your unit as to what you should and should not put into it. The manufacturer knows the limitations of the unit and passes this knowledge to you through those instructions.

3. Never use hot water when using the disposer. Always use cold water. Hot water melts fat and allows it to flow through the drain pipes. As the fat cools during this trip, it may cling to the sidewalls of the pipe and solidify. Eventually this will cause a blockage in the pipes. Cold water, on the other hand, solidifies the fat. The disposer then grinds it into solid bits which can be carried easily through the drain pipes.

4. Before doing any work on a disposer, shut off the current in the disposer circuit. Do this by removing the circuit fuse or by tripping the circuit breaker to OFF. In some cases, disposers are plugged into wall outlets, and you cut off the current by unplugging the unit. Power must be cut off to guarantee that no one accidentally starts the disposer while you are working on it. Such an accidental start can cause severe injury.

How it works

Each disposer has an upper and a lower chamber. Garbage is stuffed down the throat of the disposer into the upper chamber, where it falls on a rotating table or flywheel. The flywheel has on it two or more small pivoted hammers, which lie flat when the flywheel is at rest, but which fly outward and revolve when the flywheel is spinning. They toss the garbage against the sidewall of the upper chamber.

A metal ring with teeth in it, called a shredder, is built into this wall. The shredder rips the garbage into tiny bits. These bits are washed down the drain by a flow of cold water.

Some disposers are continuous-feed, and others are batch-feed. The continuous-feed type has a rubber baffle plate over its mouth, through which garbage is fed. It is controlled by a wall switch. Once you turn this on, you continuously feed garbage into the unit until the job is done. Great care must be taken to see that you don't allow your fingers to go down through the rubber baffle while the unit is operating.

The batch-feed models have a cover which must be in place before the unit will operate. In this type, you feed a batch of garbage into the unit, fit the cover into the mouth and turn it. The cover activates a switch which turns on the unit. When the first batch has been disposed of, you remove the cover and feed in the next batch. This unit is safer because there is no way to get your fingers into the upper chamber while the unit is in operation.

What can go wrong

There really isn't much that can go wrong with the average garbage disposer. It is ruggedly built and has only a few moving parts. The biggest source of trouble is jamming—the result of overloading the unit or putting material into it which it wasn't designed to take. Once you remove the jam, the unit operates once again.

It is possible that there will be failures in the motor. Experience has shown that the life of the average unit is from five to ten years, and that if the motor wears out or burns out, it is usually more economical to buy a new disposer than repair the old one.

There are several switches in each disposer, and switches are subject to wear. Therefore the switches are sometimes a source of trouble. As a rule, you can buy a replacement switch, remove the old switch, and install the new one. However, it is important to get an exact replacement. When ordering a new switch, take the model number and the part number to the dealer.

The switches include the on-off switch mounted on the counter or wall near the unit for continuous-feed models, and the on-off switch mounted in the neck of batch-feed models. Some units have another on-off switch in the cold water line that works in conjunction with the other on-off switch. Its function is to assure that the disposer won't operate until cold water is flowing. Check your owner's manual to learn which switches your unit has and where they are located.

The overload switch

Many garbage disposers have an overload switch which shuts off the current when too heavy a load is imposed on the motor. This switch usually trips to OFF when the unit becomes jammed, and thus saves the motor from burning out. If your unit has an overload switch,

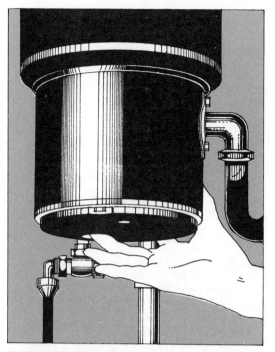

THE FIRST THING to do when your disposer fails to start after a jam or an overload is to locate the overload switch. Wait several minutes, then press it to reset the safety circuit. Some disposers have an automatic resetter and no button. Others have buttons on the side of the unit.

OVERLOAD SWITCH

know about it and know where it is located. Otherwise, you may not be able to start the unit after clearing a jam, and may assume that the motor has burned out when it has not. Many a service man has made a repair call only to discover that the only problem is an overload switch in the OFF position.

On some later models, the overload switch automatically resets itself after about five minutes, during which time the switch cools off. With switches which must be reset manually, wait five minutes before pressing the reset.

Clearing jammed units

When a disposer jams, it stops grinding. In most jams, you can hear the motor humming as it attempts to drive the unit. What you hear, of course, is the motor being overloaded—a situation which is relieved when the overload switch shuts off the power after about 30 seconds.

Important: Remember to cut off the current to the disposer circuit before starting to work on the jam. It is not enough to depend on the overload switch to keep the disposer turned off. When you have finished working out the jam, remember both to reset the overload switch *and* restore current to the disposer circuit.

A disposer jams when some type of material prevents the flywheel from returning. To clear the jam, it is necessary to remove the material. Some units have an automatic reverse-action switch which kicks in automatically after a jam. Very frequently, the reverse action will loosen the clogging object. Other units have a manual reverse-action switch. With these units, the first step to take following a jam is to flip this switch.

If the reverse-action, either manual or automatic, does not clear the jam, then you must fish out the jamming object. *Do not attempt to do this until you are absolutely certain the current in the disposer circuit is off.* With the current off, use long-handled tongs to fish the jamming object out. It may be necessary to use a long screwdriver as a pry bar to move the flywheel backward a bit to free the jamming object.

Remember that when you have cleared the jam, you must return power to the circuit and reset the overload switch. When the jam has been cleared, the disposer should work without difficulty. Jams seldom damage the disposer.

Motor hums, but disposer doesn't operate

POSSIBLE CAUSES	WHAT TO TRY
1. Garbage is jamming the unit	If your unit has a reversing switch that switches flywheel direction, causing the unit to spin in an opposite direction and dislodge particles, use it. If not, reach into the hopper and try to turn the flywheel counterclockwise by grasping an impeller and using it as a handle. If you have a special wrench that some manufacturers supply to help clear jams, use it. If nothing works, unscrew the bottom housing from the upper housing, but be careful not to let the bottom half drop. It is heavy. Remove obstructing particles from below.
2. Bearings are frozen	Remove the bottom housing and try to turn the flywheel. If it binds (not because of jamming waste), replace the flywheel and motor bearings if they are accessible. If they aren't accessible, you will have to take apart the entire unit, including the motor, to reach them.

Motor shows no life

POSSIBLE CAUSES	WHAT TO TRY
1. Tripped overload	Relieve the heavy load and press the overload reset relay.
2. On-off switch of batch-feed model has shifted	See that the stopper engages the switch when it is locked. If it doesn't, reposition the switch so it is in its proper place.
3. Burned-out switch	Check all switches for continuity with the switch turned on, but make sure the disposer is not connected.
4. Burned-out motor	Direct-test motor with a line cord. If it doesn't show life when the cord is connected to its terminals and plugged in, dispose of the disposer.

Disposer won't shut off

POSSIBLE CAUSES	WHAT TO TRY
1. On-off or cold-water switch is stuck	Replace the switch.

Disposer shuts itself off

POSSIBLE CAUSES	WHAT TO TRY
1. Tripped overload switch	Relieve the heavy load and press the overload reset relay.
2. Defective overload switch	Remove the lower housing to get at the motor and replace the switch.

Lengthy grinding time

POSSIBLE CAUSES	WHAT TO TRY
1. Impeller is stuck	Reach into the hopper and try to move the impellers. If one doesn't move, pry it up with a small screwdriver.
2. Shredder is worn	Replace the shredder if it is replaceable and if a replacement part is available. If not, consider replacing the disposer.

Disposer leaks

POSSIBLE CAUSES	WHAT TO TRY
1. Worn bearings and seals	Disposer requires a complete overhaul. It will probably be more economical to buy a new unit.

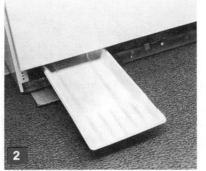

REMOVE the front grille and slide cardboard strips under leveling legs or rollers to move the refrigerator.

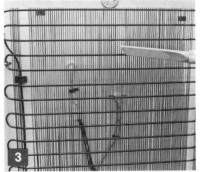

REMOVE drain pan; wash, replace. Vacuum the condenser coils under the refrigerator in a forced-draft system.

VACUUM the coils on the refrigerator back in a natural-draft system. Remove debris under the coils.

Refrigerator tune-up cuts operating costs

■ PREVENTIVE MAINTENANCE on domestic refrigerators is a safe and simple job. It helps keep the unit in good working order and cuts down on electric costs.

Before you start work, pull the plug. Nothing is more upsetting than shooting off fireworks in the refrigerator, winding a shirt sleeve in a condenser fan blade, or worse.

In most cases you will have to move the refrigerator to get at the plug. Start the move by grabbing the top front corners and rocking the refrigerator back and forth, then side to side. While rocking, pull it forward until you have enough room to reach behind it and pull the plug.

After pulling the plug, check to see if you have a natural- or forced-draft condenser. If you see black coils attached to the back, you have a natural-draft system. Forced-draft condensers are tucked away underneath, where a fan forces air over the coils.

Natural-draft condensers are easy to clean. Use a narrow nozzle on your vacuum and a dust brush. Carefully brush off dust and hair clinging to the condenser and vacuum it up.

Forced-draft condensers take a little more work to clean. Remove the front grille. With the help of a flashlight and a narrow nozzle, carefully vacuum out the condenser coils underneath the refrigerator.

The back cover is usually black cardboard with a strip of fiberglass insulation attached inside. Older models may have a black metal cover. Simply remove screws holding the cover.

Carefully vacuum the condenser fan motor and fan blade. Don't bend or warp the blade, or it will tend to wobble and wear out the fan-motor bearing.

If the fan blade is made of plastic, replace it with a metal one. Plastic fan blades tend to warp or become brittle and fall off due to the temperature in their location.

Vacuum out the rest of the dirt underneath. You should see clearly from back to front of the refrigerator, *through* the condenser coils before replacing the back cover.

The rubber seal along the inside of the door keeps heat and moisture from seeping into the refrigerator when the door is closed. A faulty seal or torn door gasket have almost the same effect as leaving the door open all day.

Wash accumulated dirt off the gasket with warm soapy water and carefully inspect it for rips. Also wash around the door frame where the gasket closes against it.

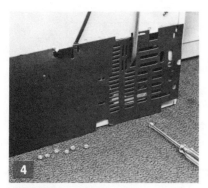

UNSCREW and remove the back cover; clean it with a vacuum. The cover is often cardboard, sometimes metal.

CAREFULLY VACUUM the condenser fan and the fan blade. Remove all dust and debris from the area.

LOOK FOR worn or torn door gaskets which let heat and moisture enter even when the door is closed.

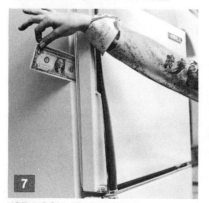

USE A DOLLAR bill to check proper gasket seal. You should feel tension when you pull on the dollar.

USING a hair dryer and a towel, carefully defrost the freezer. A dishpan can be used to collect melting ice.

DRAWING OF REFRIGERATOR locates condenser coils, fan and motor. Make certain that these parts are thoroughly vacuumed.

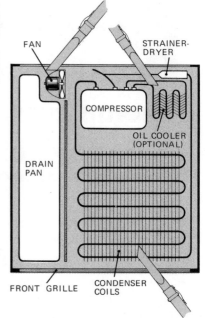

Use a dollar bill to check for proper gasket seal. Close the bill between the door and door frame. Slowly pull it out. If you feel tension, the seal is okay. Do this all around the gasket.

There are several ways to correct a seal leak. Fix small leaks by gently heating the gasket with a hair dryer and stretching it to fit. Lift the gasket and check to see that it is screwed in place. Larger leaks can be remedied by adjusting hinges so the door fits evenly.

Cracks in plastic door liners are among the easiest things to seal. While it is not good in places that must be rigid, an instant rubber caulking compound adheres well and keeps moisture from soaking into the insulation between the liner and outer door shell.

Frost buildup in the freezer acts as an insulator and reduces the freezer's ability to absorb and disperse the heat of the food inside. Defrosting used to be a messy, time-consuming job. Today you can defrost an inch of ice in 15 minutes using a hair dryer—if you elect to consume the needed electricity.

Move food to the refrigerator section. Place a towel on the freezer bottom to absorb water and put a dishpan on a convenient spot on the floor. Turn on the dryer to its hottest setting and melt a spot of ice on the top of the freezer, holding the dryer at a 45° angle so water won't drip back into it.

As the ice melts, gradually work the hair dryer in widening circles. Don't let hot air hit the plastic directly. Use your fingernails to loosen slabs of ice gently. *Never* use metal or hard plastic to scrape off ice.

Wash the freezer with warm, soapy water and ammonia, rinse and dry. Plug in the unit, turn it on and the tune-up is complete.

CUSTOMARY TO METRIC (CONVERSION)

Conversion factors can be carried so far they become impractical. In cases below where an entry is exact it is followed by an asterisk (*). Where considerable rounding off has taken place, the entry is followed by a + or a − sign.

Linear Measure

inches	millimeters
1/16	1.5875*
1/8	3.2
3/16	4.8
1/4	6.35*
5/16	7.9
3/8	9.5
7/16	11.1
1/2	12.7*
9/16	14.3
5/8	15.9
11/16	17.5
3/4	19.05*
13/16	20.6
7/8	22.2
15/16	23.8
1	25.4*

inches	centimeters
1	2.54*
2	5.1
3	7.6
4	10.2
5	12.7*
6	15.2
7	17.8
8	20.3
9	22.9
10	25.4*
11	27.9
12	30.5

feet	centimeters	meters
1	30.48*	.3048*
2	61	.61
3	91	.91
4	122	1.22
5	152	1.52
6	183	1.83
7	213	2.13
8	244	2.44
9	274	2.74
10	305	3.05
50	1524*	15.24*
100	3048*	30.48*

1 yard = .9144* meters
1 rod = 5.0292* meters
1 mile = 1.6 kilometers
1 nautical mile = 1.852* kilometers

Weights

ounces	grams
1	28.3
2	56.7
3	85
4	113
5	142
6	170
7	198
8	227
9	255
10	283
11	312
12	340
13	369
14	397
15	425
16	454

Formula (exact):
ounces × 28.349 523 125* = grams

pounds	kilograms
1	.45
2	.9
3	1.4
4	1.8
5	2.3
6	2.7
7	3.2
8	3.6
9	4.1
10	4.5

1 short ton (2000 lbs) = 907 kilograms (kg)
Formula (exact):
pounds × .453 592 37* = kilograms

Fluid Measure

(Milliliters [ml] and cubic centimeters [cc] are equivalent, but it is customary to use milliliters for liquids.)

1 cu in	=	16.39 ml
1 fl oz	=	29.6 ml
1 cup	=	237 ml
1 pint	=	473 ml
1 quart	=	946 ml
	=	.946 liters
1 gallon	=	3785 ml
	=	3.785 liters

Formula (exact):
fluid ounces × 29.573 529 562 5* = milliliters

Volume

1 cu in	=	16.39 cubic centimeters (cc)
1 cu ft	=	28 316.7 cc
1 bushel	=	35 239.1 cc
1 peck	=	8 809.8 cc

Area

1 sq in	=	6.45 sq cm
1 sq ft	=	929 sq cm
	=	.093 sq meters
1 sq yd	=	.84 sq meters
1 acre	=	4 046.9 sq meters
	=	.404 7 hectares
1 sq mile	=	2 589 988 sq meters
	=	259 hectares
	=	2.589 9 sq kilometers

Miscellaneous

1 British thermal unit (Btu) (mean) = 1 055.9 joules
1 horsepower = 745.7 watts = .75 kilowatts
caliber (diameter of a firearm's bore in hundredths of an inch) = .254 millimeters (mm)

1 atmosphere pressure = 101 325* pascals (newtons per sq meter)
1 pound per square inch (psi) = 6 895 pascals
1 pound per square foot = 47.9 pascals
1 knot = 1.85 kilometers per hour
1 mile per hour = 1.6093 kilometers per hour